T0381387

BESIEGED BIAFRA, FROM THE EYES OF A TODDLER

Uche Ugochukwu Agbugba

authorHOUSE·

AuthorHouse™
1663 Liberty Drive
Bloomington, IN 47403
www.authorhouse.com
Phone: 833-262-8899

Published by AuthorHouse 05/29/2024

ISBN: 979-8-8230-2503-4 (sc)
ISBN: 979-8-8230-2484-6 (e)

Library of Congress Control Number: 2024907190

Print information available on the last page.

This book is printed on acid-free paper.

UNTOWARD

Death came,
ran after us,
with cruel determination,
unwilling and early graves
came to the rescue.

The hangman,
stood grotesque
determined to loose
the blades of the guillotine
over our hapless necks.

We ran still,
pelted from the sky,
that made our huts
shiver in the hotness
of the day.

Our tears
fell sadly upon the wet earth
flooded with blood..
Their hands
on our neck
by brothers we
had dined and wined..

Uche Ugochukwu Agbugba
2024.

PREFACE

Many years after the Nigerian Biafra civil war, I could be likened to one imprisoned with recurring thoughts, by scenes and events that characterized the civil war. The events of those days even though I beheld them as a toddler, are not lost in the labyrinths of my memory.

God blessed me with a good memory to remember most things that we went through in the war. I recall vividly too, the things we suffered in those days of anomy when common sense and our sensibilities failed to make us take our hands away from each other's throats.

The events, scenes, and thoughts of those dark days, I have put on paper as I saw from my perspective for all to read and have an insight into what the rest of us went through in those very dark days. It shows our fears, death in low and high places, starvation and the general absence of the things that sustains life.

As I said earlier, I believe my account would open the gate of a different perspective of the conflict that sought to scatter the contraption of the British colonialists headed by lord Lugard called Nigeria and show its unworkability even in her much-laboured existence.

That the war took away three years of my life and the likes of me is not a matter for debate. Our overall and eventual development as a country, individuals, and a people suffered unduly on the alters of hatred, ethnic jingoism, immaturity, and from the overall fact that we as Africans appeared to be unable to effectively come to the grasp of managing our affairs, taking our overall fate in our own hands and steering towards a positive and progressive future. The surprising cases of colonialism and slavery prove the assertion.

The days in the conflict we had to run, always scared me beyond any imagination that words could ever explain. The sound of shelling and other sounds of heavy gunfire were very unwelcome disruptions of our tranquility, our sense of peace, and a rape of the sanctity of our God-given life. These and others struck untold terror and cast a shadow of death over us always.

These events and their period unrepentantly stole the period I was supposed to be rollicking in the sand. The time I was also supposed to be without a care in the world, eating whenever I wanted to, was however spent in the wild, running from enemies I did not know when I made them and eating lizards and shrew as my source of protein to forestall my legs being swollen by kwashiorkor. This lies in the innermost part of my life that I would never forget.

I still remember and miss my childhood days which glory I lost in the war. The days I was supposed to be running into the arms of my father or mother whenever they came back from work, sleeping in their bosom when overcome by fatigue, was directly turned to fleeing with them out of harm's way.

As we fled, we stepped on those who had died as we hastily made good our escape. We prayed under our breadth that we be not like them as they lay forlornly in agony and many in death upon the face of the earth.

I was constantly afraid because when I looked at my mother's face, she looked terrified of what might happen next that was surely going to be negative. Instead of being well fed, my eye sockets were deeply sunken and my scapular had holes that had resemblances to that of a skeleton. This was as a result of wide spread hunger that was deliberately put in place to bring about a capitulation and subjugation. My ribs were exposed and countable as a result. As a scarecrow hung and dangled in the wind, so did my dress. My eyes glowed surreptitiously from a big head by a thinned-out skeletal body. I was even lucky to be this way. I saw countless other kids who died and were abandoned when they became too big a burden to be borne by their bearers in most cases their parents, whose lives too were equally without any guarantees.

I saw my mates devoured by the merciless kwashiorkor. Their distended stomach and broken legs cried for attention that only shallow graves hideously answered.

The circumstances surrounding the outbreak of hostilities where the Igbo were massacred in great numbers and an eventual shooting war have been confined to history as a 'pogrom'.

The reasons and circumstances that necessitated the war and the unleashing of this senseless mayhem upon a people are there for all to see.

All I knew and still remember today was how my life and those my age were disrupted by the war, how my mum grabbed me and my two brothers (my younger sister having died earlier in the war) and headed towards the back side of our kindred that led us to a road that facilitated our gateway to safety.

This came about because, suddenly in the hot afternoon of a certain day in 1968, when the sun was high up in a clear blue sky, there was an outburst of gun fire. Upon this, commotion and confusion broke out as everyone ran for dear life. This was how I lost my slipper.

I still remember it vividly. It had a white sole with blue straps. I was compelled or rather was prevailed upon by my mother to throw it away because it had matched countless mounds of excrement that clung on it, and apart from the immediate encumbrances of locomotion, we could not spare any second to remove the excrement.

The sound of gunfire was getting closer and closer behind our backs. Even when I tried amid the confusion, my hands touched and were smeared terribly with a smelly mixture of excrement I had matched along as we ran.

It will not be out of the way to say at this juncture that I got used to abnormalities and was mired in them in the war situation. We were acquainted with them and no longer treated or regarded them as they were. We were no longer normal without their unobtrusive companionship. Our lives consisted of and were complemented by them. Even calmness or serenity was regarded with a lot of suspicion. It was always like a situation before the storm. It was an unhealthy one. We were more comfortable and more at home with the real storm, and the sound of war. It sat well on us like a cloth we have worn for a long time. Such was the time we had during the war.

The unkindest cut of all was my kid sister. She died from gastro entireties. That this otherwise treatable sickness claimed her, bore testimony eloquently to the deliberate and untoward absence of Medicare in the Nigerian civil war on the Biafran side.

If I do not write down on paper the events of those days, they will surely be lost forever. It is why I have written this simple prose narrative.

All that is written down in this narrative is based on the real and actual events witnessed by the author as a toddler. The characters and their names are the real names of the members of my father's house. The towns and villages mentioned are their real names.

CHAPTER 1

THE UNEASY CALM

In the dry season of 1968, when it looked like the sun came up earlier than in the past, when the rays streaked through the crevices of the two small leaved wooden windows embedded in the thick mud walls of my father's house, crept into my sleep, dazzled and woke me up.

It heralded the coming of another day in my small village called Ama-eze Obibi-Ezena in the South East of Nigeria. In addition to other things that concerned our days we had to grapple with, was the apprehension that hung in the air suspended by the news of the war. This we awaited to make landfall like a category 4 storm that barrelled towards our shores.

I slept by the window on our grass-stuffed mattress for the simple reason that I became the last child in a family of four children one more time, my younger sister Chinwe having just died.

We were a family of six: father, mother, and four children. The children consisted of three boys and a girl who did not make it out of the fratricidal war, for it claimed her. She was sadly the only one out of my immediate family it claimed.

In the manner of seniority, the eldest is called Mba-nugo. He is soft-spoken and dark and about 1.6m in height. He is shy and not given to being noisy or extroverted. He possesses the qualities of a gentle soul.

My older brother was called Chika. He was the direct opposite of my eldest brother. He was more aggressive, vibrant, and highly extroverted. He was also pugnacious and fought his way through any jam. He commanded a lot of respect among his peers and below. He was often times called 'Hitler' because of his ability to have his way by force or outright coercion. He died in 2005.

Our sister Chinwe was the only one we were made to have in the manner of her sex. She was like a pearl that dazzled from the dust of our time. She was a rising star whose brightness was forced down from focus before it even had the chance to further captivate. She was mother's consolation that she had one like her kind. Her death in 1968 was very devastating to her.

My father was called Adolphus Canice Manukaji Agbugba. He came from Amaeze Obibi Ezena of Owerri North LGA in the present-day Imo State of the South East of Nigeria. He was born in 1919, the third child of my grandfather who was called Agbugbakanshi.

My grandfather, Agbugbakanshi was a wealthy man. He had a barn full of rows of choice yams like 'ese-ese' and 'nkokpu agwa' as my people termed them and an appreciable number of acres of arable farm lands. This however drew the envy of his kith and kin. His wealth made it possible for him to be polygamous.

My grandmother, Nne Uche, was the last of the two women he married. She died early in the early 1930s of unknown causes but probably of heart failure, of failure to have a larger share of my grandfather's attention. She did not have any formal education and was a junior partner in the polygamous setting in my grandfather's house.

My grandfather also did not have any formal western education. Even with the advent of the British and their culture from 1894 to 1960 according to (Encyclopedia Britannica).

He did not consider it worthwhile going to acquire the Whiteman's ways or his education which was termed 'Western'. It was considered a wasteful venture and exercise in futility something that the 'Efulefu', the dregs of the society, outcasts were punitively pushed to acquire.

My Father told me that while working in the forest for my grandfather, cutting it for farming, he usually ran away from the forest to attend school which the white man had set up when the dry monotone bell of school tolled, slowly and dully.

It called the natives to school to be educated in the white man's ways. My grandfather did not believe in this because of cases of flogging and their brand of discipline which was not our way. He believed that his children should not be subjected to this kind of odyssey.

However, the closest he came to the white man and his form of enlightenment was the few times he became a porter to him and helped carry his colonial luggage to Port Harcourt. He scorned the white man totally and hated his ways.

I don't know the circumstances that surrounded my grandfather's stint in the colonial service, the very people he abhorred. I do not also know if his services to the colonial lords were out of coercion or otherwise.

He saw them as spoilers who came to turn our society upside down and change things and our perspective of life in general. If not so, how could the white man with all the knowledge and advancement he claimed he possessed, merged different people with different languages and cultures into one country in the ill-fated amalgamation of 1914, other than the claims of administrative convenience and selfish interests?

This set up a background for the civil war that claimed the lives of many people years after the amalgamation.

According to (Chinweizu, 2006) in a paper presented at Muson Center, Onikan, "It was an orchestration that was designed to fail." The Lugardist states as he called them, Nigeria inclusive, "were a contraption that was not to be and a perpetual appendage for manipulation and exploitation." He opined that states set up by lord Lugard in what was termed 'Lugardism' are a false framework. "This has therefore predisposed these states, Nigeria inclusive as having the wrong foundation for building African power."

Such schemes and/or thoughtlessness were what my grandfather abhorred which made him not have anything to do with them.

(David Laitin,1986) in his book, "Hegemony and Culture..." further stressed that Nigeria was a structure initiated by former colonial powers which had neglected to consider religious, linguistic and other ethnic differences.

Nigeria which gained independence from Britain in 1960 had at that time a population of 60 million consisting of nearly 300 different ethnic and cultural groups. It was surely against common sense except for the ulterior motives of the Whiteman who was not concerned about the stability and wellbeing of their contraptions.

It was surely a well-thought-out recipe for disaster. It was like a time bomb ticking away to a destructive explosion. It did not take long to come. It was like a dark shadow that was cast upon the hapless people of the geographical area called Nigeria.

However, the contact with the white man rubbed off on my grandfather in a way for he named my father 'Johnson', the name of the man whose load and burden he bore through the footpaths to the coastal city of Port Harcourt. He was so impressed with it that he reserved it for my father and duly named him after the colonialist.

My father who was called English names Johnson and Adolphus, was the second son of my grandmother Nne Uche. His only brother Ndu-ka-uba was the first. He died quite early having been poisoned early in his life. My grandfather's other wife in this polygamous setting was Nne Uluocha. She was the mother of my Uncle, Thomas, and others.

Uncle Tom was the most prominent of my grandfather's household. He was a prison warden in the colonial service of the British in Obubra in the present-day Cross River state of Nigeria. He took my father there in 1933 where he attended government middle school in the way of the colonialist educational system.

My father was however smart and clever. So, in 1933, he left home and went to Obu-bra at the instance of his half-brother Uncle Tom. When he finished middle school in Obubra, with the dearth of people who were educated in the white man's way, he went into teaching and became a pupil teacher in Naze of present Owerri North LGA.

While the colonial administration in the 1940s where firmly in the saddle of affairs of the state of Nigeria they created, palm oil contributed in no small way to the colonial economy as oil was taken to Britain as a contributor to the ongoing industrial revolution.

According to (Aghalino,2000. p.19), the Industrial Revolution in Europe in general, and Britain in particular, created a demand for oil palm produce from Nigeria and other parts of Africa for various purposes.

Also, according to (Watts, m. 1983) in the book; (Silent violence; food famine and peasantry in Northern Nigeria), Palm oil was used as lubricants for trains and other machines, for the manufacturing of soaps, candles, margarine, and as cooking fat. It was also used as livestock feed.

According to (Helleiner, 1966). It was against this backdrop that palm oil and palm kernel were some of the earliest commodities exported from Nigeria by the British even before the formal imposition of colonialism in the country.

There were oil mills that dotted the landscape of the South East. This processed and produced palm oil for export to the home country of the colonialist.

My father worked in one of these, especially the one at Owerrinta in present-day Abia state in 1953 having left his job as a pupil teacher. This was a year before the coming of the Richard MacPherson constitution in the growth and eventual march of Nigeria to self-determination.

He married my mother shortly after, who was also called an English name, Teresa. On the verge of Nigeria's independence, he joined the Eastern Nigeria public works department in old Onitsha province from 1959 till the creation of East Central State when a shooting war broke out.

We became aware as children born to our parents in Onitsha. My father was posted here according to his career as a roadman in the Eastern Nigeria civil service. It was from here, while our lives were just beginning to bud that we had to run to our village in the South East of Nigeria in 1967 when the war started.

My father was not a tall man. However, what he lost in height he gained in comeliness and intelligence. He was a handsome man; his thick moustache conspicuous from afar distinguished him plainly upon a chocolate complexion. And so, it was that he met my mother who was called Teresa in 1954 and they married. My mother came from Ama Awom kindred of Owerri town the present capital of Imo state in the South East of Nigeria.

She was the daughter of Silvanus Nwere of Ama Awom kindred of Owerri. He was a policeman. He was separated by a year or two from being referred to as having been a policeman in the West African frontier force.

My parents were Christians and staunch Catholics, the religion of the Whiteman that was soon embraced by many. My mother was more zealous than my father in this new religion. She was training to be a Catholic Reverend Sister at Eme-kuku in the 1950s before she met my father and her ambitions were permanently scuttled by my father's overtures which resulted in an eventual marriage. She was a business woman all her life and combined her business with her roles as a mother and housewife fairly well.

Ours was a model family even as we were growing up and getting to know our parents better. My two brothers' Mba-nugo and Chika were older than me. I was in the same manner of seniority older than Chinwe, our youngest sister, who later died in the war.

We were living in Onitsha where my father worked as a roadman with the Eastern Nigeria Public Works department between 1963 and 1966.

I remember how peaceful and calm everyone was. I was 6 years having, born in 1961. I had started school for my hands could then go over my head to touch my ear on the other side of my head. It appeared to be the only yard stick by which schools age maturity was known and measured. And so, it was that my father enrolled me in one of the county council schools in Onitsha. We were living at No 18 New American Road in what I now understand was a middle-class neighborhood of Onitsha.

As each morning came, my parent's driver after I was made ready for school, drove me to school in our Fiat 123 car. My brothers also went to the same school. I recall only my enrollment as the days came. We were picked up again when it was afternoon, when the sun was high above the head.

I came home to launch and rest for the day. Siesta was strictly observed in our house. I remember us running to our rooms to feign sleep when it was time to observe siesta and we were not asleep yet. Dad came to our room to see our eyes firmly shut and allegedly asleep. He assumed we had gone to sleep. He went out with some satisfaction. This was like our everyday life and the routine thereof.

With our mongrel dog, Billy, we awaited my father's return from work in the evening with a lot of expectation. This was so that we would eat the roasted cashew nuts he always bought and also eat the leftover of his food he usually remained.

It had become a routine. We looked towards it with a lot of expectation. I, Chinwe, and Billy, our mongrel, played in front of our flat. With Chinwe's tricycle, we had fun-filled days.

Despite all the peace and normalcy that pervaded, something seemed not right and terribly out of place. A certain ominous dark cloud wafted over the horizon of the 'Lugardist state' called Nigeria barely 6 years after her independence from her colonizers; the very independence celebration that was celebrated with so much fanfare.

But as for us, 6 years after, I and my brethren whose lives were beginning to bud, had our overall fate hidden in uncertainty and gloom. We were stopped from going to school all of a sudden. Mum and Dad discussed in very pensive tones with moods of concern and worry on their faces about the political situation in the country.

According to Frederick Forsyth in his book (The Biafran story 1969), events and situations in the country were indeed spiraling out of control toward a possible war.

The political atmosphere in the country had become charged with corruption among the ruling class, destroying the essence of self-determination as independence that Nigeria had gained.

The confidence and trust of the populace in the government had so waned that apathy was the answer to the affairs of the state. Events as they unfolded showed that we have not yet acquired the maturity to run our affairs four years after independence for in the 1964 general election, it became sadly obvious.

The 10-year alliance between the NPC and the NCNC was broken by Sir Ahmadu Bello. He announced that the Ibos have never been true friends of the North and never will be. This resultantly made him form an alliance with Akintola who was firmly in control in the west. According to Mr. Forsyth in (The Biafra Story 1969), it appeared an alliance with a southern party would be necessary to keep his lieutenants in power at the national level in Lagos. He therefore found a pliable ally in Akintola than Okpara.

With this alliance, NNA was formed which is the party of Ahmadu Bello's NPC and Akintola's. With this development, NCNC had no other option in her political life than to get along with the Action Group, the remnant of the party who had remained loyal to Awolowo who was in prison. And so, it was that UPGA (United Progressive Grand Alliance) came to be.

The electioneering campaigns were not encouraging at all as it was all dirty and lacking in gentility and what electioneering campaigns ideally ought to be. The NNA campaigns in the west were largely based on racial bias and slurs. It hammered and dwelt on 'Igbo domination' in the socio-political affairs of the country. This however prompted the president of Nigeria Dr. Nnamdi Azikiwe to make appeals for fair electioneering campaigns and warned also of the dangers of whipping up racial and tribal sentiments.

Up North, the UPGA candidates were molested by NPC thugs when they tried to campaign. According to Mr. Forsyth's, (The Biafra story, 1969), UPGA candidates complained they were either prevented from registering or even after registering, their NNA opponents were returned unopposed. With the entire atrocious events prelude to the election, it was thought and was greatly in doubt if the election would still hold. But it went ahead with UPGA boycotting for obvious reasons. This gave NNA victory at that election.

The president though unhappy with the provisions of the constitution in this regard, asked Balewa to form a broad-based government. This calmed events that would have caused trouble for the young country only four years old. This was in 1964.

In February of 1965, federal elections came, held in the East and the Midwest. UPGA made an appreciable impact getting 108 seats while the National Alliance won 197 seats. The brouhaha generated by the February election had barely died down when preparations for the November elections in the western region began.

In this election, premier Akintola was defending his appalling records of governance and a continuation of his position. If that election had been fair, and because of Akintola's unpopularity, it would have made UPGA to win in the west and Lagos. This would have invariably given UPGA control of the upper House while leaving the lower house to the National Alliance.

Akintola was in no doubt aware of this and confident of the support and of course the backing of powerful Ahmadu Bello in the north and of Prime Minister Balewa. He was therefore emboldened. Confident of impunity with the support of the two men, he went ahead with the election procedure.

UPGA having been advised by the federal electoral body, tidied up the nomination of their candidates well before the day of the Election. But it was surprising therefore to see the 16 Akintola's men including the premier himself declared winners because they were unopposed. What followed was like a script from hell according to Mr. Forsyth. Electoral officers disappeared, ballot papers vanished from police custody, candidates were detained, polling agents were murdered, new regulations were introduced at the last minute but only mentioned to Akintola's candidates" (The Biafra Story, 1969)

And so, it was as they counted the votes, UPGA agents and candidates were kept out of the collation centers. This was perfected by the government-employed police according to Mr. Forsyth. Some UPGA candidates however by some miracle were declared elected by the returning officers. With instructions being that all returns should pass through the premier Akintola's office, and so it was, while western radios under Akintola reeled out different names, the radio of the Eastern region gave out also different names it claimed came from the returning officers.

According to the Western Government, Akintola had 71 seats and UPGA 17. He was resultantly asked to form the government. UPGA objected and claimed it had won 68 seats and that the election had been tampered with. This was easily believed by observers because of obvious widespread discrepancies. Adegbenro who was the leader of UPGA was forming his government based on what he thought was the election result. He and his supporters were promptly arrested.

This brought trouble as anarchy reigned according to Mr. Forsyth. "Murder, arson, looting went on ingloriously. On the road, gangs of different political affiliations cut down trees blocked the roads, and demanded the political leanings and affiliations of motorists. Answers that did not meet their expectations received instant jungle justice." (The Biafra Story, 1969)

Despite all the killings and the mayhem that went on, the Prime Minister was quiet and did not move a finger in rebuke or any affirmative action. Despite calls and pleas to him to declare a state of emergency, dissolve the offensive Akintola government, and order fresh elections, he declared that he had no power.

One wonders about the kind of politics of intolerance that our leaders played. Opposition was ruthlessly pushed to a point of destruction other than a display of sportsmanship. Ethnicity and racial tendencies ruled and let intolerance speak with the pendant havoc on the people, peace and progress of the entire people also tampered with.

Nigeria which had lighted the hope of the colonized independent Africa was tethering on the brink of disaster and was about to scatter even as the world watched with dismayed disbelief. The Prime Minister in an act to present a smokescreen to the world that all was well with Nigeria hosted the Commonwealth Prime Ministers conference in Lagos in the first week of 1966 to discuss how to restore law and order in Rhodesia (South Africa).

It was ironic that while dignitaries arrived and the Prime Minister shook and welcomed his international guests with broad smiles at the international airport at Ikeja, a few miles away, Nigerians were dying for the army had been called in to quell the riots.

The riots however could not be quelled by the army and by the insistence of the General Officer Commanding, Major-General J.T Aguiyi Ironsi, the soldiers were withdrawn.

A peep into the army then showed that a majority of the infantrymen were from the middle belt. The Tiv riots were still for the army, the majority of whom were from the Tiv ethnic group. They could not be used against their kinsmen. The army therefore proved ineffective in the face of riots in Tiv's homeland.

The same way they were not of use in the Tiv riots was the same way they proved ineffective in the west of Nigeria. Their sympathy lay not with Akintola's regime who was an ally of Sardauna of Sokoto, the persecutor of their homeland. They tended to show sympathy for the rioters being themselves in much the same situation as they.

It became obvious that something had to give by the second week of January 1966. The state of the country was at the precipice of complete anarchy. And so, it was that on the 14th of January, a group of young officers decided to clean the Augean stables. It was so serious and determined that within a few hours, Sardauna of Sokoto, Akintola, and Balewa were dead and so was the first republic.

And so, it was that on the evening of the 14th of January a highly idealistic Major Chukwuma Nzeogwu an Ibo of Midwestern extraction, who had lived all his life in the north, an erratic chief instructor at the Nigerian Defense Academy of Kaduna led a small detachment of soldiers who were mostly Hausas out of town ostensibly on a routine exercise. Upon arrival at the splendid residence of Sardauna, he told the soldier that they had come to kill him. There was no objection. Later Major Nzeogwu said that if they had objected to his point, they would have shot him. They had enough bullets in their guns.

They stormed the gate of the Sardauna's house, killed three of his guards and lost one of their members in the fight while in the compound. (The Biafra story, 1966)

In the compound, they shelled the place with mortars. It was with a grenade Nzeogwu used to break down the main door injuring his hand in the process because he came too close. Sardauna was killed along with three of his servants.

As this was going on in the residence of the Sardauna of Sokoto, elsewhere in Kaduna metropolis another group entered the house of Brigadier Ademolegun and killed him with his wife as they were still in bed. A third group yet came on Sodeinde who was second in command at the Defense Academy. This was the last of the killings in Kaduna.

On the 15th of January, Chukwuma Nzeogwu spoke from Kaduna Radio. He told his listeners that the enemies they were fighting were political profiteers' swindlers, men in high and low places that let bribery thrive and demand ten percent and seek to perpetually divide the country so that they can remain still as ministers and V.I. Ps (The Biafra story 1969).

While in Lagos even as the situation was changing rapidly in Kaduna, Lagos was also not left out. The execution of the coup in Lagos was in the hands of Major Emmanuel Ifeajuna. He was of Ibo extraction and had a taste of fame as an athlete.

After dark, he drove into Lagos with truckloads of soldiers from Abeokuta barracks. Small detachments like platoons were dispatched to all parts of the city in search of their objectives.

Three officers of northern origin died. This included Brigadier Maimalari who was commanding the second Brigade, Lieutenant colonel Pam, the Adjutant-General, and Lieutenant Colonel Largema, who was commanding the fourth battalion. They were respectively killed in their homes while Largema was cut down at the Ikoyi hotel where he was staying.

Major Ifeajuna went after the politicians. The prime minister was arrested in his home. According to Mr. Forsyth, he was bundled into the back of a Mercedes Benz and was made to lie on the floor. Okotie Eboh was the finance minister from the mid-western region of the country. He was shot at his home and his body was dumped in the boot of his Mercedes car.

They went after the Igbo minister of trade Dr K.O. Mbadiwe who escaped across open gardens to an empty state house. The soldiers did not bother looking in this place and Dr. K.O. Mbadiwe was spared.

The last casualty was an Igbo officer Arthur Unegbe. He was in charge of the ammunition store at Ikeja barracks. He was killed for refusing to hand over the keys of the armory to the dissident soldiers.

The execution of the coup in Ibadan was however carried out with dispatch too. Here, the obvious target was the premier. At his house, the dissident soldiers were met with a volley of automatic rifle fire. According to Fredrick Forsyth, soldiers stormed his house. He was dragged out and finished off. At another location in Ibadan, Fani

Kayode was arrested. It seemed so far that the coup had gone according to plan. It seemed the dissident soldiers had consolidated but it was short-lived.

No man did more to foil the coup than the G.O.C, Major General Ironsi. It seemed he was also destined for death that night. He had been at a party given by Brigadier Maimalari. He left for another party at a boat moored at Lagos docks called Aureol. When he got back to his house at midnight, his phone was ringing and it was Colonel Pam to say that something was going on. Later, after the phone call Colonel Pam was dead.

Ironsi's Hausa driver came in to tell him that something was going wrong. The Major General moved quite fast. He ordered his driver to drive him to Ikeja barracks which was the biggest Army barracks. He was stopped at a roadblock mounted by Ifeajuna's soldiers who promptly pointed their guns at him. Ironsi fearlessly got out of the car and thundered at them "Get out of my way." (According to Biafra story, 1969) They gave way and he sped off into the night towards Ikeja barracks to rally against the coup.

When he got to the barracks at Ikeja, at the sergeant majors 'quarters, he rallied the garrison and set in motion counteractions that eventually saw the defeat of the coup. And so, it was that he backed orders almost all through the morning. Troops that were loyal to him took over. Major Ejoor reported before dawn and was ordered to get back to Enugu to take charge as the second in command to Colonel Fajuyi who was away on a course. Major Ejoor went to the nearby airport and took a light plane to Enugu.

While there have been some successes for the coup plotters in Lagos, Ibadan, and Kaduna, Ifeajuna, and Okafor realized there was no one to take charge of Enugu, and decided to go to Enugu by road 400 miles away in a Mercedes Benz car.

Ejoor arrived in Enugu and took over the garrison overtaking Ifeajuna and Okafor driving below. He immediately withdrew troops from the premier's house. It was ironic that later in the day at 10 am the same soldiers stood guard of honour as a fearful Okpara said goodbye to President Makarios of Cyprus who came visiting. This was how the coup was foiled in Enugu. Okpara left for his town Umuahia. (The Biafra story, 1969)

In the Midwest, the coup plotters arrived at the premier's house at 10 am that morning but were withdrawn at 2 pm on the orders of the G.O.C who was fast regaining control of the situation.

It was obvious the coup had failed. Ironsi had re-established authority and control. Ifeajuna and Okafor on arriving in Enugu saw Ejoor already on the ground. According to Mr. Forsyth, Okafor hid in the house of a local chemist and Ifeajuna ran away to Ghana but later came and faced his fellow plotters in prison.

The first coup in the country had started and ended. It was not however bloodless as could be seen. As at the last count, the premiers of the North, west, and Prime Minister were dead. Among the senior officers were three Northerners, two westerners, and two Easterners another Ibo officer was killed because he was wrongly perceived as being one of the coup plotters.

Also, a handful of civilians including the wife of Shodeinde, and some house help of Ahmadu Bello's household. Also, about a dozen soldiers were killed.

While Ironsi had re-established control, Kaduna was still in the hands of Nzeogwu. A throng of cheering Hausas ransacked the palace of the Sarduana. Major Usman Hassan Katsina, son of the Fulani Emir of Katsina, sat beside Nzeogwu at a press conference before Nzeogwu had named him the military Governor of the North. Ali Akilu the head of service offered his support to Nzeogwu. But Nzeogwu's influence and hold on the state of things were waning and fast.

Ironsi was in charge of Lagos and the rest of the south. Though he was the reason why the coup was foiled, he did not lose sight of the fact that the coup enjoyed some popular support of the masses of the country according to Mr. Forsyth.

And so, playing on the side of caution, he asked the acting president to appoint a deputy premier following the demise of Balewa on Saturday 15th January 1966 from whom he Ironsi could take valid orders. This was not however done until Sunday morning when the cabinet finally met. Ironsi made it clear to them that he could not ensure the loyalty of the officers and men of the Nigerian Army unless he took over the reins of power.

According to Mr. Forsyth, Ironsi was very right. It was said that even the soldiers who did not take part in the coup would not accept a return to civilian rule of the thoroughly discredited politicians.

Events had further deteriorated. Nzeogwu realizing that his colleagues in the south had failed in their respective roles took a column of troops and headed south until he reached Jebba on the river Niger. If the garrisons in the South were split between those for and against Nzeogwu, a civil war would have been the only way out.

By the 15th of January, before midnight Ironsi broadcast from Lagos that since the government had ceased to function, the armed forces had been asked to form an interim military government and that he 'Iron side' Ironsi had been invested with authority as head of state of the Federal Military Government.

The Army obeyed his orders. Nzeogwu withdrew to Kaduna barracks from where he too emerged to go into custody. The new regime started well.

I have taken time to throw some light into the events of those days that made us be at dagger's end and each other's throat. It is painful to think that it could all have been avoided. The lives and destinies lost and destroyed could have been avoided also. The country would have been better for it. The properties lost in the ensuing confusion could not have been so if common sense prevailed.

According to Mr. Forsyth, Ironsi however committed blunders for which he is still being remembered today and which are too obvious to ignore. He did not try the coup plotters as the relevant military laws demanded and by the advice of Northern and Western officers. He did not heed the calls to try the coup leaders but went boldly ahead to subvert the constitution and its succession stipulations. He suspended it in the mind that it was to be made stronger and better for a return to democratic rule.

CHAPTER 2

THE COUNTER-COUP

The Nigeria press further aggravated an already sour situation and being dominated by the south, made caricatures of the killed Northern leaders in a cartoon on the 29th of July 1966. This was irksome as Northern soldiers in Abeokuta barracks mutinied and gave birth to a counter-coup with Gowon emerging as the head of the Supreme Military Council despite Murtala Mohammed's opposition and claims to the seat. It was however given to Yakubu Gowon because he was from the minority and a Christian.

The military governor of the Igbo-dominated South East, Colonel Odumegwu Ojukwu, citing the northern massacres and electoral fraud, proclaimed with the southern parliament the secession of the South-eastern region from Nigeria as the Republic of Biafra, an independent nation on 30 May 1967.

Although the very young nation had a chronic shortage of weapons to go to war, it was determined to defend itself. Although there was much sympathy in Europe and elsewhere, only five countries (Tanzania, Gabon, Côte d'Ivoire, Zambia, and Haiti) officially recognized the new republic when a shooting war commenced according to Fredrick Forsyth's (the Biafra Story 1969)

Several peace accords, especially the one held at Aburi, Ghana (the Aburi Accord), collapsed and the shooting war soon followed. Ojukwu managed at Aburi to get an agreement on confederation for Nigeria, rather than a federation but was warned by his advisers that this reflected a failure of Gowon to understand the difference and, that being the case, predicted that it would be reneged upon. When this happened, Ojukwu regarded it as both a failure by Gowon to keep to the spirit of the Aburi agreement, and a lack of integrity on the side of the Nigerian Military Government in the negotiations toward a united Nigeria. Gowon's advisers, to the contrary, felt that he had enacted as much as was politically feasible in fulfillment of the spirit of Aburi. (The Biafra Story, 1969)

The Eastern region was very ill-equipped for war, outmanned and out-gunned by the Nigerians. Their advantages included fighting in their homeland, the support of most Easterners, and determination. The UK which still maintained the highest level of influence over Nigeria's highly valued oil industry through Shell-BP- and the Soviet Union supported (especially militarily) the Nigerian government. (Awoyokun Damola's 'The Untold Story of Nigeria's Civil War', 2013)

I remembered my father eyeing his Zibala-named double-barreled gun in the process of war breaking out. I believed every other man in the East had the same feeling and disposition.

The UK and the Soviet Union supported (especially militarily) the Nigerian government while Canada, Israel, and France helped the Biafrans. The United States seemed to be neutral but helped the Biafrans through the Red Cross. (Awoyokun, Damola, 2013)

The stage was all set for war, the drumbeat of which had become so deafening and frightening. Even as a child. The times were becoming confusing and requiring urgent actions and decisions. It was wishful thinking that a shooting war would not come. The countless numbers of the Igbos that came in truckloads, who escaped being killed and with decapitated bodies of their kith and kin accompanied, stirred up wailing and loud lamentation among the people in the east.

According to Justice G.C.M Onyiuke's report of the tribunal ('Massacre of Ndigbo in 1966) Report of the Tribunal,) "Between 45,000 and 50,000 civilians of former Eastern Nigeria were killed in

Northern Nigeria and other parts of Nigeria from 29th may 1966 to December 1967. Although it is not strictly within its terms of reference, the tribunal estimates that not less than 1,627,743 Easterners fled back to Eastern Nigeria as a result of the pogrom.

How about the numerous officers whose only offense was because they were Igbo, who died, summarily executed?

According to Professor Ruth First in (The Barrel of a Gun; The Politics of Coup d'état in Africa.) "Within three days of the July outbreak, every Igbo soldier serving in the army outside the East was dead, imprisoned or fleeing East wards for his life." It was like all hell was let loose, especially on the Igbos.

As a child, I still recall a magazine that had 'pogrom' on its cover page. The inside of the magazine contained macabre images of decapitated bodies, and wounded men and women in different stages of wounding. I and my brethren flipped through its horror-filled pages of bodies that were decapitated, of limbs that were cut off from their bodies. The most bizarre I saw in that magazine was that of a pregnant woman whose belly was cut open and the contents spilled. Others yet were seen on mammy wagon trucks in different stages of afflictions with wounds and bandages all over as they headed home to the east. It was bizarre. We looked at the horrible images on the pages of the 'pogrom magazine' oblivious of the severity of what was going on in the country we lived in.

With these recent events in the country, the very bases upon which the unity of the country stood were being dealt a deadly blow if there was even anything like it. The bloodletting occasioned by the second coup did not in any way suggest any form of fraternity or something closest to it.

This was borne out by a statement obtained from "The Problems of Nigerian Unity; The Case of Eastern Nigeria, 1966)' *"recent events have shown even more clearly that the belief of the easterners that only a strong central authority could keep the people of the country together was presumptuous, and perhaps an oversimplification of the situation. Now, the whole basis on which the easterner's conception of one nation, one common citizenship, and one destiny was built, appears never to have existed."*

It was mutually agreed even among the different federating units that the case of Nigeria as a country was a fatal accident of history that the British orchestrated and midwifed. The units themselves knew that it was so. Even in the political life of the country, it has been like a do-or-die affair to clinch political power and hold on to it as long as possible to the exclusion of the other units. But what pains me most today as an adult is the fact that we are still in pursuit and defense of the falsehood that we can live together and can make the unification a lone role model of its type in a world that God made every tribe to be on their own as the tower of babel typified. We have continued to kill each other and suppress opportunities once it's not from the tribe of them in authority.

Even the northern region had submitted an article about their thought on Nigerian unity in a (memorandum submitted by the Northern delegates to the Nigerian ad hoc constitutional conference), Lagos, 12th September. 1966.

> *"Recent events have shown that for Nigerian leaders to try and build a country for the future on rigid political ideology will be unrealistic and disastrous. We have pretended for too long that there are no differences between the people of this country. The hard fact that we must honestly accept as of paramount importance in the Nigerian experiment, especially for the future is that we are different people brought together by recent accidents of history. To pretend otherwise would be folly."*

How could we explain to posterity that we lost our kith and kin because we willfully suspended the incongruous reality of our disunity and its glaring adversities and dwelt on the pretenses of such? How could we have swallowed the bait of oneness as a people that had at best become illusionary and totally nonexistent, letting the blood of our compatriots flow freely and a puddle formed of it?

My parents watched events as they unfolded with great fear and apprehension. There was fear and apprehension among the Igbo. The killings had been gruesome and had instilled fear in all of us. Among my dad's friends who came around our house then, it was the topic of the day as they talked with pain of the twist in the existence of the Igbo man. It was my mother that made me know we were going to be hounded like animals in the wild and killed. It was a source of fear as we pondered upon the information and the fate that awaited us in the entity called Nigeria.

The mayhem in other words bloodletting was so determined that it was time for us all to go. If we were going to be killed, was it not better we died where we all came from, in our respective homesteads other than elsewhere?

To the east was like the clarion to get out of harm's way and await the same death in our respective homesteads.

And so, my family must go too. Though, we were in the eastern heartland already. Our place was farther away from where the battle was being set in array.

So sometime in 1967, my mum put us in our Fiat saloon car and we headed to Owerri to my father's village in the southeast of Nigeria. My parents were determined to stay there and await death and its scythe by the hands of them that pursued us. My father stayed back to continue his work in Onitsha until such a time it became impossible to do so.

In the early days of 1968, when the war had started, our routine was expectedly disrupted. We slept with our hearts in our bare hands literarily. Fear and apprehension took over our lives.

Tragedy struck my family in the early days of the war. My only sister, Chinwe died of a treatable sickness called gastro entireties. With her death, I became the last child in my father's house one more time with all the rights and enviable privileges accorded the last born.

After my sister's death, I was eased back into this position I had left when she was born. I did not however understand fully the circumstances surrounding the death of my younger sister; they were hidden from me by age and mum.

All I knew was that she took ill and complained of stomach pains and could not stand erect. Her light-skinned body became pale and gaunt. She was in some great pain that neither Mum nor anyone close or far away had answers to.

It was painful seeing one's daughter in death throes and you were not able to do anything. So was my mum. She stood helpless and watched as life flowed out of her only daughter because she could not do anything to save or help her. The girl before her death, suffered without any help coming her way.

Out of desperation, Mum took her to a local spiritual church in our village. In my opinion and hindsight, this desperation worsened Chinwe's case.

When she came back, she became worse. It broke my heart to see my younger sister in such pain and distress and nothing was being done to help her. Her strength continued to fail until she died four days later. Because of the war, there was no visible healthcare system. There were no medicines to be administered. Everything was in a state of utter hopelessness.

My mother was the only one with us. My father was not around as was said and was not always around during the days of the war. He was contributing in the war effort. As a road man, his skills were needed for the war effort. So, my mother was all alone taking care of the family with some obvious disadvantages.

She tried to save Chinwe amid nothing. She went from pillar to post but could not get help to save her only daughter.

The war was beginning to take its toll and had claimed immediately a member of our family.

The scarcity of food was already becoming the order of the day. Salt had trickled to a stop like water from a tap that the source had broken or cut. Food was cooked without this basic condiment. Meal times were nightmarish. Chinwe was hardest hit.

We (my three brothers) forced ourselves to eat lizard which ingloriously graced our unsalted meals. We ate anything Mum presented before us and which we found ourselves. But Chinwe could not bring herself to eat those things we were eating. The mere sight of us eating lizard made her want to vomit. She questioned their unwholesomeness as edible things. But it held the solution to our escaping the trap Kwashiorkor had set all over the Biafra's enclave.

The unsalted meals and the lizard meat in tow made Chinwe miserable indeed. Most times, Mum pleaded with her to eat but she looked away in great sorrow and sighed resultantly. She was gravely worried about her only daughter and my only sister.

We were still receiving some relief materials which were shared with us before now. The connections Mum had with these people who were agents of the relief body, ensured we got some vital relief items in the form of dried egg yolk, milk, stockfish that was wet and salty, corn meal, and others.

At such times, Chinwe came alive again. Her appetite improved and she ate as much as was placed before her with voraciousness. It was in these circumstances that Chinwe licked too much milk and dried egg yolk which made her sick.

There was no medication given because there was just none. There were however a few attempts to drive away the 'evil spirits' that were allegedly claiming her soul in one of the spiritual churches in our village as has been said. That failed too and more like accentuated her death. It was purely what drugs and medication could take care of and not what some unnecessary foray into the spiritual realm could solve.

Such was the situation Mum faced. She watched as my younger sister died in her arms without any help of any sort reaching her. She was inconsolable. She cried like Rachel in the Bible. She refused actually to be comforted because her only daughter lay in her hands in death.

I did not however understand fully well the implications of death, no thanks to my age. That I was not going to see her again, that I was going to miss her even as I write were foggy and by no means clear. I still behold her pretty, spotless, and innocent face with her snub nose fitted perfectly on her chocolate-complexioned face that was heavily dimpled when she attempted to smile.

I still visualize the last walk she made by the paved corridor of my father's hut when Mum scolded her because she could not get up from where she was lying down. Mum insisted and she got up from where she was lying down and did the walk that I still see today.

She walked with a shaky gait like one walking on a tight rope. It was a deathly walk. She was bereft of strength as was associated with life. Her eyes were dull and like some light that was flickering out. She walked towards Mum for no particular reason.

She wanted to convince herself that her daughter's sickness was not as bad as it seemed. She stared in utter helplessness as her eyes shut in death four days later.

When she departed by death and was buried, where my father's house now stands, a vacuum was sadly and resultantly created. Mum was inconsolable as the stories of the war were becoming very frightening. She cried like I had never seen her cry before. She broke into ululations as tears streamed down her middle-aged face.

She bemoaned her fate and the day that had brought this misfortune upon her. Even as a child, it confused me but brought tears to my eyes as my mother's words and tears made my tears flow too.

I cried not only because mum was crying but also because Chinwe was my only sister and we had rollicked in the sand together as playmates and not only in playing but also in bickering. I looked over her too like a lion would to a lion cub even as young as we were in a practical demonstration of the man in me and my tenderness for my kid sister.

Now all those were gone with an evil wind that swooped down and carried her away like a kite would to a chick.

I remember sympathizers streamed in to sympathize with Mother. She sat on a mat in the living room devastated. They told her to take heart in the absence of any other tangible admonition. Others lamely said that it had happened and that there was nothing anyone could do. And such clichés that filled the air around the bereaved were no different in ours. We were literarily pelted with such words and statements that tended towards boredom.

She looked however sternly at each person as if she wanted to identify who it was that inflicted this pain on her. Others sat by our side in a true show of emotion, saying nothing particularly but made my reacquired position by Mum's side quite uneasy and uncomfortable.

But in this whole melee, I discovered that I regained the place by my mother's side, as 'nwa nkpalaka' a position my kid sister had naturally occupied. It looked as if people consoled us together. It seemed too that I was again part and parcel of my mother like a kangaroo and the baby in her pouch.

It seemed too I was the greatest succor she needed at this time. It pleased me somehow that I played this noble role as mum's pacifier despite some salient infringements upon my overall rights of growing up as a boy.

She kept me close and held me firmly too. Like a priced trophy, I was clutched and held in such esteem. She looked over me a couple of times to ensure my vital signs were still there and promising.

She was in real agony and fearful of what the future had in store for us her children now that one had ingloriously kicked the bucket. Something she had seen far away from her had come into her own house. She was thoroughly baffled. Even now I think my mum brought me closer so that death would not also snatch me away.

After my sister's burial, I and my mother did not sleep in our house. My mother's sister who became such by the lone fact that she came from the same kindred in Owerri as her, took us to spend the night in her house. This was to reduce my mother's grief or in obedience to some tradition. It was apparent Mum did not trust my father's people, which was why we went to sleep in the other kindred called Okwu where my mother's sister resided.

Wherever mother went, I followed. It was not what I wanted for myself but was dragged along by her. This was the new regime that the situation brought about.

As the days went on, we fell back into our daily routine. My sister's death had pitifully but surely paled into insignificance. That was too how I came to be sleeping by the side of the window of my father's house.

With the passage of time mother recovered and the rest of the things that revolved around her rallied too. And so, it was that we went again into the drudgery of life in my father's village. The stream of people that came to sympathize with us had since dried up altogether.

We slept in the night and woke in the morning. I forgot about my sister and moved on with the rest of my life by looking for lizards and learning to set traps for rodents. Our lives were also facing severe challenges from the war that was going on.

In this position I reverted, I was not bothered with waking up as early as others. I was left to sleep more until the sun crept in and woke me up. I moved away from the sun sleepily and stretched myself almost to breaking point and the day had started for me.

It was no longer news that war had broken out. As a kid, I did not need any more reminders that there was a war going on. The whole place was replete with signs and effects of an ongoing shooting war. While a series of meetings and efforts at mediation had failed to stave off the war, the battlefield became the place where the matters were being settled.

But for us in my father's village of Amaeze Obibi in present-day

Owerri North LGA, South East of Nigeria, the battlefields of the war seemed so distant for us to be bothered for now.

We had relocated from Onitsha where the echoes of it were almost deafening in 1967. In our village in the southeast of Nigeria, we thought we were far away from the eye of the storm.

Our lives went on normally like nothing was in the offing other than accounts of how the war and stories of one maltreatment or the other on our Igbo brothers and sisters. We still went to the farm in the morning and came back in the evening. Our sustenance depended upon what we got from the land and so farming in those days was given some pride of place.

My duty on the farm was planting melon and maize. It did not require much physical or mental exertion which was why I was asked to do it.

Mother always drummed it into my ears that I placed three seeds, well-spaced into the earth before covering it again with earth. She taught me also how to place them. This I did on the farm with the sun high above beating us without mercy.

The breeze at times blew reluctantly, trees and leaves also moved with the same reluctance. Birds chirped excitedly in the forest nearby. The bolder ones came closer to where we were working and chirped more excitedly as if they mocked our efforts. There was this one we called 'tiri- tiri' -the wren. She always perched on a shrub nearby and chirped boldly and loudly. From the chirping we assumed it challenged us, we interpreted their chirping as;

'Tiri-tiri'
'I gbagbufu m,
I gbagbufu m'
(Can you kill me,)
(Can you kill me?)'

We were most times unable to kill it as she boasted to our hearing. This was because the wings beat faster than most birds her size. Before you could raise your catapult, if you had any, the bird hurriedly flew away into the bright sunny day. We could not kill her. She was given the name 'tiri-tiri' because of her chirping. And also because of the way we thought she challenged us.

Work at the farm however continued in a very boring routine. My brothers; Chi-ka and Mba-nugo, being older, continued to till the impoverished earth to lay the cut cassava stems on it. Mum being a strong personality, insisted on seeing her instructions carried out to the latter.

The cassava stems were cut to size by Mum to ensure they were equal in length and eliminate any other discrepancies. And also, to avoid any unforeseen that might make them grow inwards or worse still become stunted as the village people dreaded.

Our lives depended to a large extent on the proceeds from the farm. The war made it imperative that farming in those days was taken seriously. The harvest from our farms too included mainly cassava which formed the basis for the production of garri, our staple food.

So, its production or cultivation was not toyed with and was very serious business. This therefore required the attention of our mother to oversee this area which required extra carefulness.

My brothers and I, therefore, laboured the day away on the farm irrespective of the fact that we never lived in the village and were not used to the hard life and ways therein.

We were variously born in the stations where my father worked as a roadman in the Eastern Nigerian public works department before the advent of the war. So, village life and farm work were to a great extent strange to us, at best punitive the way we were made to work.

But with the coming of the war and the impending hardship and scarcity, we had no choice but to till the impoverished earth to earn a living. Mother told us that we had no one to do it for us, so we had to do it for ourselves. Our black bodies glistened in the hot afternoon sun with sweat all over us.

I was used to fighting a little gnat called 'Ohuhoro'. I took time off to fight this insect. This gnat specialized in flying very close to your ear or eyes, attracted by the odor of sweat or only what she knows. It usually launched into your eyes if you were not vigilant. This then required you to ask for help, to blow out the gnat from your eyes. But I did not understand why it always wanted to get into my eyes.

It informed me that she had come by flying close to my ear with a high-pitched sound like the mosquito. At such times, I hit the gnat to kill it but only hit my body. The insect usually resumed the quest to lick my sweat or continued in her attempts to enter the eye.

At times under the intense sun and the hardship of farm work, one of my brothers wanted to ease himself. I went along with him. In so far as it was going to take us out of the tedium of farm work, I looked forward to it. At such times, we headed for the bush at the end of the farm. I never missed such opportunities of getting a respite or some rest.

To the forest, we disappeared. My elder brother Chika was very good at these excuses and gave it more often than our eldest. He always wanted to ease himself and I always followed for reasons I have told before.

In the forest, he climbed on top of a shrub, one with extended branches, and began to defecate. I too followed. I found for myself a similar shrub and climbed to do as he was doing. When we were done, we looked for some special leaves that were rough other than those that were smooth which we usually cleaned ourselves with.

There were wild berries and fruits around us but one known as African velvet tamarind we called 'Nchichi' was predominant. The farming season was its season. We climbed one tree of Nchichi after another looking for one that was sweetest and which was not 'slapping our cheeks' with distaste.

And Mother's voice reverberated from the distance, bringing us back to the routine we had come to hate.

We darted from the bush and came back to work with more than a handful of 'Nchichi' which we licked intermittently as we tilled the earth and sowed corn and melon seeds. Mum always said that if you continued to go away to defecate unduly, your work still awaited you.

"Nwaa, nyucha otulaoye,
 oru ya no chereya."

She always warned us with this proverb. And truly we still had our roles waiting for us; my melon sowing and my brother's cassava planting.

At a time, we became hungry. Mum with our help prepared food we came to the farm with. The food was usually eaten when we were hungry so that we could carry on till sundown. Even my position as a toddler did not change that. I ate when everyone else did. I was always worn out by hunger.

The gnat did not help matters either as there was an unending quest for my sweat and eye. It even went into my eyes sometimes and I had to beckon on one of my brothers that was close by to blow out the gnat from my eyes.

It added to my annoyance despite the hunger that was beginning to make me stagger and see doubly.

I always wondered about the food that waited by the shade under a shrub, why we could not just eat instead of an indeterminate time that only mum knew and why life could be this hard.

'Nwankwo le eri ngwere', the falcon 'cried' from a nearby location. She was always in the habit of stalking her prey. As the name implies, it eats lizards mainly and chicks that their careless mothers left unguarded.

But as far as I was concerned, the 'cries' of the falcon reminded me how hungry I was and in need of food. It also reminded me of the emptiness of the time and the deep yearning for better times. The falcon's cries therefore painted this picture vividly for me.

She was always well at home with her cries that drenched the whole place and period with a certain dryness that I still hear today. I always searched the trees nearby to catch a glimpse of the falcon but did not always see it.

Eventually, food was brought and we washed our very dirty hands with little water and remained enough for drinking. Our hands were not properly washed but we ate with them all the same. It presented an image of one washing with spittle.

Mum dished the soup and the pounded yam. The pounded yam was made from yam seedlings. It was reserved for days we went to the farm. It formed part of the rare days we were treated to this choice or delicacy of pounded yam and Ofe Owerri soup.

Mum gave instructions to my eldest brother on how well to pound the yams. She told him to add some oil to it. So, when eventually it was served on the farm, it had become so hard that it looked like it had crystallized again. It became so strong that I thought it had gone back to its original form.

And so, we broke it down a bit in a clenched fist and swallowed in hunger. Our eyes closed momentarily at each swallow because of the hardness of the pounded yam that struggled and scratched through the esophagus into our hungry and empty stomachs.

It was also of some concern to us and doubtful too that the disappearing mound of pounded yam was going to fill us as it got tucked away variously into our hungry mouths.

The soup was usually 'Ofe Owerri', made from pumpkin (ugu leave), dry fish, oil, water, pepper, etc. At this time in the war, it was deficient in a lot of the required and usual ingredients.

Such ingredients as stockfish, which we called 'okporoko', dried catfish, and okazi were not readily available because of reasons associated with the ongoing war.

As the meal was hungrily swallowed, we were allowed to rest for about thirty minutes before resuming our work at the farm.

The farm upon which we were working had been cleared after it was left fallow for five years. During this time, the land was left to replenish. Farming was done somewhere else because there was a lot of arable land for cultivation.

So, this one we were farming on had been left for five years. It had grown quite wild. So, getting it ready for farming meant it had to be cut down and burnt when it dried. The burning made room for the next step in the farming cycle. This therefore came with the burning of the trees that provided shades one could stay under to avoid the scorching sun.

The only places that were spared were under palm trees that escaped the burning by fire. But the palm trees were too tall to offer any meaningful coverage from the sun. And so, we virtually stayed under the hot afternoon without much covering as we tried to rest. For me and my elder brother, we went to the end of the farm into the forest nearby.

As evening finally came, the sun turned a deep golden yellow way down in the horizon obscured with trees. It was time for us to go home. The sun had finally gone down and for me, it made me think that the war between the sun and the earth had ended at least for today.

The sun going down signaled the end of proceedings for the day too. I looked forward to leaving the farm and heading home to catch up with things I was forced to abandon for the farm.

As kids, we were told about spirits, especially the wicked ones, and how they tormented humans especially the erring and the cruel ones. I was also told that spirits came to take over the farms after we had gone. And woe betide any human who stayed back after sunset. So, we were told as we had a peep into the nether world and the spirits.

I was filled with happiness as we gathered our things- hoes, pots, plates, and seeds. We gathered all these and collected some half-burnt sticks as firewood my two brothers carried. I was left to carry the plates and the other things we used to eat with.

In my mind, I always felt that some wicked spirits were already watching from the bush at the end of the farm. I wanted us to get away in a hurry. I had the corner of my eyes beamed that way, determined not to be taken unawares by any spiritually induced eventuality. It was said by Shakespeare that it is the eyes of childhood that fear the painted devil.

On the pathway home, we looked grotesque, darkened by contact with sticks that were half-burnt by fire in the burning of the farmland earlier. This we called 'Agwakaochu'. The blackness of the charcoal was so pronounced that we grotesquely walked home being covered with it.

We licked the velvet tamarind 'nchichi' we plucked in the forest near the farm. With our loads balanced on our heads, we used our hands to break it and lick the fruit.

This was a feat I learned in those days. Before now it was not possible to balance the weight on my head without it tilting over. But now, I was good at balancing. I followed my brothers and left my load on my head and plodded along with my 'nchinchi' on my hands and in my mouth proudly.

We had no immediate cares or concerns about anything. As we walked home after the work on the farm, we were happy to have finished for the day and were graciously homebound. Mother on her part cut some leaves for our lone goat that bleated at home in anticipation of our return and the food that was sure to follow.

On one or two occasions, we beheld a big rodent 'Odu' dart across the pathway. Chika my elder brother taught me that at such times I should stop or move back to observe what happens next, a hungry snake might be in hot pursuit.

This was what we experienced in the village. It was a jungle scene. The whole scene played out before us. We watched with keenness and a certain fear of being drawn into the melee.

As we got closer home, the sound of mortar and pestle in their traditional romance reached our ears. Columns of smoke went up having escaped from the thatched roofs of the huts in the village on this windless evening. It informed of them who had gone ahead to the next huddle of the day: that of cooking which we all must do as eventide ensues. It was also good information for us as matches were scarce and we needed to go where the fire was already burning to take coals of fire to make our own at home.

So, Mother at such times told us to "Jebiaoku" "go and bring fire." from such places where smoke was seen ascending out of the thatched huts in the village.

On this farming day, some folks had already come home and were preparing the evening meal. As we got home, we dropped our farm implements and sat for a short while to rest having been exhausted by working all day in the farm and having walked for a kilometers and half from the farm.

At home, we faced a different kind of challenge. We had neither pipe-borne water nor any other water source other than rainwater and one from the "well". The water that remained in the earthenware that had two or more wriggly mosquito larvae was scooped up for my mother to bathe with.

Water was so scarce in the village that we did not waste it at all. It was highly treasured and much sought after. It was almost as precious as the food we struggled to have.

Pipe borne water was like a luxury heard of in the pages of stories of distant lands. We trekked kilometers to neighboring villages with (ebela) 'calabash' just to fetch a liter or more of stream water which we treasured highly. 'Ura muru ukwa' stream at Eme-ke Obibi was the one mostly visited. The older ones carried steel buckets we called pails.

As we set off from home to the stream, and on our way back, the buckets were covered with leaves to prevent the water from pouring out while walking or when one broke into a trot to get home faster for the distance was quite long.

Some who still had bicycles, made it to the stream by this. Three tins on a wooden platform were made to stay at the back of the bicycle. It was hard work riding with this load strapped at the back of your bicycle.

Someone asking for a cup of this water usually believed the water came out of the mouth of the fish and said 'Give me this water that just got off the mouth of a fish.' We treasured the stream water highly for it came at a great cost and it was clean, or so we thought. It was therefore reserved for drinking only.

The well was therefore the only source of water supply for the entire village for domestic use. There was no stream cited in the village by nature. The village was not blessed with this resource. Rainwater filled our troughs during its season. But afterward, it was with great effort that we got water. This was the reason why we were taunted by surrounding villages as a place of extreme dryness, where the impala's head hit the dry floor.

This is an Igbo proverb that connotes a place of extreme dryness and infertility as a result of the unfortunate absence of a sure and pure water source.

The well which then became our only source of water was dug by the local authority of the Eastern Nigerian Government. The well was very deep and was almost close to one hundred feet in depth. Despite this, the water was not drinkable. The rope used to lower the buckets into the well made the water unfit for drinking. Parts of the rope broke off and fell into the water below.

It required a lot of effort to draw water out of the well.

The people laboured to get water from this singular source. It was here that our only source of water was situated. It was here that the whole village gathered to jostle for space around the small perimeter of the mouth of the well to draw water. It was here too that we came.

And so, we left for the well to fetch water for our evening meal and bathing. The whole village had gathered to fetch water for their respective domestic needs. It was worse than a market situation because of the disorderliness and struggle that reigned.

Everyone shouted above his or her voice to overcome the sound of the buckets that hit the concrete wall of the well as they made their way down to scoop water.

It was not a place one should be after having worked all day at the farm. After much haggling and struggling, we got water. We filled our containers and headed back home.

Supper was prepared before night fell so that one would be unable to see the back of his hand. It was usually yam porridge. We ate hungrily and happily that at last, the toiling for the day was over.

Despite the apparent peace and tranquility in our village, there were stories of war raging in places like Nsukka and a place we were told was called Garkem- the border town between Cross River State and Benue States. It was the initial days of the war.

The Aburi meeting and other efforts at mediation by all having failed to settle the differences and demands between Ojukwu and Gowon, the situation in the country turned from bad to worse.

Mother always heard how the war was going on because People always came to give her updates on how it was progressing. She got informed about how things were either in our favor or otherwise and what was happening generally.

After supper, it was always a good time for us children to hear stories, moonlight, and real war stories. Instinctively, I knew the war was not favoring us with the sorrowful countenance upon my mother's face. She talked in low tones as if she did not want any other person to hear,

"Is it the truth?"

She always asked the person talking to her. At such times, as I watched them, I knew it was not well with our troops and our bid for self-determination. But it was not all about defeat or all tales of victory. There were also tales of gallantry, of smart strategies which the enemy had no answers for. But for us kids, we ran off in twos to play in the moonlight;

Oro o!
Nwoke o!
Nwanyi o!

And we were formally summoned for the night's moon plays. We ran off to hide in appropriate and inappropriate places.

The moon smiled at us or so it seemed and equally played tricks on us when it hid behind clouds suddenly and threw the whole place into pitch darkness. You could see one walking and reached out only to discover that it was the mere effigy of darkness. Fireflies moved and flew about eerily in the dark in this dawn of our misery.

The moon usually reappeared and looked like it was laughing at the seeming tricks it had played. The moon's reappearance was always a time of refreshing as the whole place became aglow again with moonlight.

The trees and images resplendent in their silhouette that the moonlight created made us afraid of what we did not even know. Fireflies held sway momentarily but faded again in the fleeting brightness of the moon light on a cloudy night.

And so, our games went on. With the running and physical activity, we became wet with our dirty clothes the scarcity of water did not let us wash always. We did not even care about it. From one game to another and the moon playing tricks on us intermittently, the night however continued and got deeper and deeper.

Our plays then turned to sitting close together; we sat side by side in a circle. One person in the middle had the task of finding who had the pebble that was making the rounds in the circle. This we called 'Ese'.

It was a source of real joy as the one in the middle of the circle looked at everyone to see who had the pebble that was making the rounds behind our clenched fists.

We told stories too. We heard stories about tortoise. We learnt from the didactic nature of the stories especially when told by an older person of how life was going to be lived. Amidst the war that was raging and fast approaching our precincts, we were still learning lessons of life from such platforms that fables and folktales provided.

Tortoise was indeed a trickster. We were meant to learn a thing or two about the tortoise ways of overcoming situations. Despite the efforts at learning about the tortoise especially, we assessed the tortoise against the wholesomeness or morality of his behaviors and were mostly filled with revulsion for her numerous tricks.

At times, some of the stories and the roles he played were simply very revolting and an offense to our sensibilities even as young as we were.

We were therefore filled with a certain level of disgust and revulsion at the character traits of the dramatis personae which was mostly the tortoise.

The moon was overwhelmed by unrelenting tropical clouds that matched steadily from the southwest, and having further gone down in the horizon went to sleep. It cut our stay short and ended the bliss that was ours for the night.

For some of us, a welcome turn of events, having worked or laboured all day at the farm, we deserved a good night's rest. It was only a fair recompense. The curtain was drawn and darkness enveloped the whole place.

I traced my way back to my corner of the house and my bed as fireflies led the way. The shrills of a thousand insects especially crickets increased and became more pronounced as our noise ceased and died away, swallowed by the darkness of the night.

CHAPTER 3

MY LOST SLIPPER
(A RUN TO THE FOREST)

And so, it was, that a day came in 1968. The sun was high up in the sky. The birds flew exuberantly and carelessly- perfecting or showing off their skills. Kites flew dutifully overhead in search of chicks that scratched the impoverished earth below in the unending conflict between them that nature brought about.

It was like a day when ants equally got extra busy and gathered all they could find and dragged same to their store bank for the rainy day that was sure to come.

The day was indeed sunny. The wind was hot and limited in volume. It was like a day people contemplated what was best to be done especially about the heat that hung in the air and discomfited everyone.

Men, women, and children alike wished for one thing, that rain fell to cool down the heat of the place somehow. It was just the beginning of the dry season. Leaves turned pale in the heat of the sun and waved reluctantly when the breeze decided to pass reluctantly by too.

Lizards traversed the length and breadth of mud and cement walls in search of ants and grasshoppers that might have perched on the walls for a brief period like coming to wait for a connecting flight in an airport.

'Nwankwo leri ngwere' (the falcon) high up on a tree looked out for lizards that were carelessly exposed to carry for food. The cry of the falcon filled the air and added to the boring monotone of the voice of the period.

Even a certain bed we called 'Oguluo' (let there be war) added to the boredom and the apprehension. The bird chirped unceasingly 'Let there be war', 'let there be war' as it sounded in our language.

And so, it was that the peace was shattered by a burst of gunfire from the northern approach to our village. We were used to gunfire in the distance. We were not familiar with or prepared for this sound of gunfire that sounded so close by. We had since heard of the fall of Nsukka and Enugu, the capture of Onitsha, and the threat to Owerri. So, in the far distance, we heard the guns boomed away. We did not have any idea that an attack was imminent, but it was at least known that Owerri was heavily threatened by the federal army. The threat came to light for us this hot and peaceful afternoon in our village.

Everything came to a confused stop suddenly. The apprehension of the moment had been translated into stark reality. Mothers yelled at the top of their voices in grave concern for their children. The men yelled in fear for their wives and other members of their families. I was nearby when my mother grabbed me and yelled for my two brothers.

There was gunfire, it was not in doubt. It was coming from the northern approach to our small village, Ama-eze. The gunfire was increasing in intensity and coming nearer. The confusion was becoming intense too. No one stayed to ask questions. Our fears were confirmed, and the war had reached our doorsteps. It was very evident.

The gun shots reverberated through the forest that surrounded our village and birds scattered in confusion too. The war we heard as mere stories had reached our very door steps. This was our first encounter with the war as much as I remember.

As from this day, things were no longer the same. Our lives were physically under threat as we scampered away for safety to ask questions later.

Mother held me by my right hand, my elder brother by her left, and our eldest Mbanugo came immediately behind. We ran as fast as our legs could go. I wore shorts, a shirt, and a slipper as we ran out of our house towards a path at the back of the kindred. We had to avoid colliding or running into others as we hurried to get away from the randomness the shots brought about.

Many people heeded towards our direction and soon the way was filled with anxious relatives trying to frantically run away. The pathway we took was before now the toilet for a family. Upon this path and around it was littered with human excrement. And so, in the frenzy of running away from the advancing and rampaging federal troops, I and others matched on countless numbers of excrement that lay littered on the ground. In the frenzy, I did not watch nor care about where I matched. My slipper resultantly matched some excrement on the ground that it was heavily laden with it.

When we emerged on the other side of the village road, my slipper was so heavy that I could not run nor walk with it. I picked it up and was amazed at the amount of excrement that was under it. I tried removing it but Mother shouted above me,

"Drop it, drop it"

She shouted at me. I did. There was no time for arguments. We ran along as I left my slipper behind.

We headed to 'Okwuotamiri'. This was our most dense forest. It is located on the west side of our village. It was also proudly owned by the people of our kindred. They fought a battle to possess it in the past. It was indeed a big tropical forest with stories of sighting of big snakes and other dangerous wild animals. The men came here to set traps. It was here we ran in to hide from the rampaging federal soldiers who were hot on our heels.

After about an hour since the first shots were heard, we were in the warm and safe embrace of Okwuotamiri- the tropical forest west of our small village.

I was out of breath and my feet were sore. I had no more footwear to protect my feet. I had started reaping the bitter fruits of my lost slipper in the fratricidal war. It dawned on me that I had lost an important part of my life. No one however paid any attention to me or the ordeal that I was going through and had to bear all through the war.

As a child, there were many things I did not know. The routine life of a kid was all that I operated. I ate and played as at when due and slept when overcome by sleep. The child only sees the smaller picture and cannot grasp the bigger picture.

So it was that I did not know that the last time my father visited home, they had anticipated this invasion as Owerri was threatened. My parents had arranged to erect a hut in the bowels of this dense tropical forest.

My father was not home with us as these were going on. He was 'cut off' as was the parlance then. He was on the side that Biafra still held and he helped the war effort in road maintenance.

He was not conscripted into the army but was an essential civilian officer. He worked in the P. W. D (Public Works Department) He repaired and maintained roads and kept them motorable. Besides at 49 years, he was not of much use to the army in combat roles. He could not come to see us at will, however. He was almost killed once as he tried to come to see us. The man who led people across the frontier; who was taking them through enemy-occupied territory by some magic somehow lost it at a point. The people he led and himself, strayed without knowing into the enemy's territory. They escaped by a hair's chance.

This magic manifested by a raised right hand that showed which way was safe for the people to pass through. It was always believed that he would always lead them away from harm's way, away from where the enemy was and home to their respective families and destinations.

So, it was while he was coming to see us, he was almost killed. It was on this trip that my parents made an arrangement and built a thatched house in the middle of the forest at Okwuotamiri. It was indeed a big surprise for me to see a hut standing in the forest in the middle of nowhere when we ran here from the village. The thatched house stood menacingly in the forest like a shrine of a warlock in the cartoons.

As we approached the thatched hut where it stood, it seemed to me like it stared back at us. It looked eerie standing so forlornly out of place in the forest. This was our abode for the next seven days.

We were three families of about fourteen people with a space of about twelve by twelve. It had no concrete floor or mud walls. What served as walls were made of palm leaves which acted as the wall? The floor was made of raw earth taken from the forest floor.

Cement was the least of the material on our minds. It was not available at all. The roof was made from raffia leaves and sticks as well. So, it was that all fourteen people crammed into this 12 by 12 room to sleep at night when darkness came.

The afternoon we ran away, we did not take anything with us that was our belongings. So, we had nothing and could not do anything about it. The federal soldiers made it so.

And so, it was that we shared this small space about fourteen of us. It was very uncomfortable.

I barely slept at night even as a child. The room was so stuffy and hot, the windows having been shut for obvious reasons of safety, being in the middle of a thick tropical forest. The odor of unbathed bodies pervaded. Farthing was a common thing that compounded the ventilation problem in the room. One heard the hissing sound of farting as it escaped into the already choked air in the very stuffy room. This made it extremely difficult to breathe. Sleeping was not only difficult but laboured. The condition in the hut made it almost impossible to have a good rest by way of sleep.

I was once awake one early morning at about 2 am. All were asleep. As I lay on the mat that formed the bed, I heard twigs being broken outside. I smelt a strong odour of an animal like when you get close to a he-goat.

As the animal or whatever it was walked past our hut and away into the night, the breaking of sticks under her weight faded into the darkness.

When daylight came, I discovered that I was not the only one who heard what transpired that night. Mother heard it too. The presence of the animal filled us with so much fear for our lives. When she told the story later, other accounts were told. Some suggested that the animal was a lion; others said it was a python that came to look for food while others said it was a hyena.

The hut was however located near an anthill, this gave a lot of credence to some of the accounts, especially the snake's account. Some said that they have been hearing the animal's noise since the first night we came into the forest. To date, we never knew what it was and I am happy to recount our experience.

Life continued in the jungle as we got into the third or the fourth day. Our belongings especially the things we needed, like pots and other utensils to cook with were fritted to our new residence in the forest like rats. This was done in the night. It was when it was safe to do so. The federal soldiers that occupied the village left for their base in the evening. It was safe again for them to return to the village in the morning.

So it was that we picked the essentials that enabled us to live in the forest. Others that were not so essential were left at home. It was not everyone that ran away to the forest. Some stayed back and lived with the federal forces.

My mother and the rest who went to the forest did not want to take chances. They left to hide in the forest and went back to the village to take whatever they wanted under the cover of darkness.

They were not swayed by the stories of peace and goodness that pervaded under this arrangement of living with our enemies. The foray into the forest was justified by all that ran because of the atrocities they heard were committed by the federal soldiers.

It was however good that many did not die in our village despite the siege.

My uncle married two wives. They never really cared about each other. They were always quarreling at the slightest provocation. So it was that in this forest, a fight broke out between the two women. The eldest wife wanted a better portion of the arrangement their husband made. The younger one insisted that it had to be done her way. Tempers rose and they started fighting.

The elders battled to separate them and feared that the furor generated by the noise had compromised our position. There was indeed commotion occasioned by these two women. We feared the worst would happen.

As feared, our cover was indeed blown as others in the forest came to find what the commotion was all about. It was then that I knew that other people too took refuge in the forest. It was a full community that had run to the forest to get away from the federal troops.

CHAPTER 4

LIFE IN THE FOREST

Life in the forest reduced us to animals as we shared their habitat. We slept early as soon as the sun went down. We could not cook in the night because we did not want the fires seen in the dark thereby giving our position away in case an enemy was on the prowl.

So, we cooked early and ate early in turn. We turned in for the night early too. The forest was not a place for playing or moonlighting games. There were spikes all around that brought a great discouragement to playing.

Snakes and other dangerous reptiles were all over the place and we in other to avoid being beaten, went in early in our overcrowded cell of a hut. Our foodstuff was taken from the village at sunset when it was obvious the soldiers had left the village.

Even though they withdrew, it did not guarantee total freedom as we had our kinsmen to contend with who had become collaborators or sympathetic to our enemies.

So, Mum and the others stealthily went into the village and came back the same. It was to avoid being followed by our kinsmen who came to identify where they entered that it might not be relayed to the federal army.

Our drinking water came the same way too. I realized later that people went to the village to bring water which we drank and other things we could not take the day we ran. So it was that mother and others used the cover afforded by the night to frit all we needed like rats to our new home in the forest.

Meals in the forest consisted of yam porridge, pounded yam, or garri with Ofe Owerri soup that had no salt. The eating of the soup had become boring because of its sickening monotony. It was eaten without the usual relish. The absence of salt had made it more boring and highly undesirable.

Yam porridge had become very boring too because of the same monotony. The ingredients of Ofe Owerri were no longer complete. Salt was gone and went with it the tastiness of our highly cherished traditional soup.

Rice was a rarity. It was not only very scarce; it was not available at all. Beans were also not available. All possible sources of protein were not available. The pleasures of eating beans or fish or any source of protein were no longer there because they had gradually disappeared.

Our meals therefore consisted of foods that were all carbohydrate-based; yam, garri with soup of incomplete ingredients, and saltless. I never drank milk nor saw any in the conflict after the brief days of relief materials.

Milk was available initially when relief agencies and other bodies brought relief materials. Mother received corn meal, salted stock fish, dried egg yolk, and powdered milk in the early days of the war. These were no longer seen as the situation became more desperate.

I was so bored with having to eat one particular type of food; yam porridge all the way. The site of it drew a long bitter sigh out of me. But it was always handy and there was no other choice. This however drew our unalloyed gratitude in the face of death from starvation.

But one day we woke up as usual. We went about what had become our established routine in the forest: going farther away from our hut to defecate, cleaning our teeth with chewing sticks, and preparing to eat whatever we might find as breakfast.

The news came that the federal army wanted everyone back to the village. The federal soldiers got information that we were in the forest. They ordered us to come back to the village or else they were coming to flush out everyone in the forest in a military style of operation.

It was the sixth day of our sojourn in the forest. The ultimatum given was an immediate one. We were expected to comply immediately or bear the consequences of failure to comply. It further went that anyone found in the forest after the expiration of the deadline was going to be responsible for whatever happened to him or her.

These were trying times for every one of us, especially my mother. She was the one on whose shoulders lay the weight of navigating us to safety and out of harm's way. And so, it was that the decisions of what to do, and where to go in these times were for her alone to decide. We looked up to her in all things. She had access to information that we did not have like the massacre of defenseless civilians by the federal army in some parts of Igbo land like Asaba in 1967. (Wikipedia)

The calls to come back home did not therefore go down well with her. She was not sure what to expect back in the village or what fate awaited us with the federal troops all over the village. She was very reluctant to take us back to the village. But she was also not going to stick out in the forest alone with us. It was said that the grasshopper that was killed by a buzzard, was indeed deaf.

We took back the things we brought from the village as we made our way home to the village from our forest shelter. It was in the morning. It was also in the full glare of the federal soldiers. We went back to our house.

Our arrival home brought us face-to-face with our enemies; the federal soldiers. I saw what the enemy looked like for the first time. They were everywhere and walked about freely without any fear. They shot fowls, goats and took whatever they fancied. No one dared raise a voice in opposition.

Even as a child, it dawned on me that something was very wrong.

The boldness the soldiers exhibited in their actions, convinced me that we were indeed besieged.

An incident took place immediately after we came back from the forest. I was picking and cracking palm nuts. I was hungry and food was really scarce. Even the yams that we harvested from the farms were almost depleted. Meals were no longer frequent anymore.

So, in the course of picking palm nuts to crack and eat, two soldiers walked into our compound. The war had depleted our stock of domestic animals. They were either killed off or battered for salt and other necessities. It was not a common sight seeing fowls around not to even mention goats or sheep. The few that still moved about were highly treasured, guarded and tended by their respective owners. It was indeed an arduous task with the occupying force around.

And so, the soldiers came in, their attention was on a small fowl that innocently chuckled and scratched the earth nearby. They heard the chuckling on the road as they passed and traced her to our compound.

On the other hand, they moved about freely, entered anywhere they wanted, and did whatever they pleased. You would not want to be in this condition. So, the soldiers took positions to catch the fowl as everyone watched with great fear. We could not say anything either for or against their actions. A word rightly or wrongly said could bring about some drastic actions that would be wholly regretted.

So, the soldiers tried to catch the fowl. The fowl proved very difficult for them to catch. When all their efforts failed, they started looking for help. There were people there when they came in initially. They did not talk to anyone nor did they afford us the luxury of greeting or recognizing our presence. When their plan for catching the fowl was not working out, they commanded everyone, the owner of the fowl also to help catch the fowl. He had just come out to find out that the only surviving fowl of his entire livestock was what had attracted this much attention. Batho was his name. Everyone looked at him to find out how he was going to help these soldiers catch his fowl, the only fowl remaining of his entire livestock.

As everyone was commanded to catch this fowl, Batho was tacitly chasing the fowl away. Every one of us knew it was his fowl. He feigned keenness in helping the soldiers catch the fowl. I thought it was unwise of him for these soldiers had guns and had nothing to lose.

When it became obvious to the soldiers that he was chasing the fowl away, one of them took out his gun and fired twice at the fowl. The fowl died instantly without any other movement. I heard the soldier mutter under his breath; "iye le nye." They put the fowl in their bag and went away loudly. Their oversized and noisy boots raised dust as they walked away with Batho's remaining fowl out of our compound.

I was scared of the loud gunshot and the effects on the fowl at such close range. It was louder than the day we ran to the forest at their coming. So, when they left, we talked about it with some amusement for many days. This kind of incident marked our days in the occupation.

There were no cars and no petrol to ride them. The cars just disappeared from the roads. Bicycles ran without tires but on bare wheels because there were no replacement for them. It was a sorry spectacle to behold bicycles that ran on bare wheels and yet laden with heavy cargoes of bags of garri to the market.

The case of the fowl was the same fate that befell the womenfolk, especially the younger ones. They were not spared. My mother used to go about with me. It was to let the soldiers know that she was married and had children.

It was also to let these randy soldiers know that she was not a young woman and therefore was off limits. It became annoying at a time because I was always in my mother's company. This cut the time I had for myself to catch a trifle or play.

My aunt, Regina as other young women were not spared. They paid dearly for being women and young. She left the house early in the morning while we were still asleep to avoid being caught or seized by these ones they called 'vandals'. She stayed in the forest till about 7; 30pm in the evening when it was safe for her to come home. She left prepared. Because of the long hours she stayed in the forest, she made two sets of the meals she ate while in the forest.

It was a source of great fear to be caught by these federal soldiers. The thought of it was revolting to us all as we believed the soldiers were associated or plagued with 'kwiri-kwata' (bed bugs).

It meant that the soldier took the woman in question and thoroughly defiled her that she was not ever going to be the same woman again. So, this exercise of going to the forest was taken rather seriously.

I saw my aunt sleepily as she left for the forest early in the morning. She woke early to cook the food she carried. She left the house before 5.30am. All the women in her age bracket were not spared this ordeal. If you were seen by the federal soldiers, you were caught and taken as spoil. No amount of pleading sufficed.

This was what the young women went through. They had their hair shaved to the scalp. They deliberately looked disheveled, and unkempt and generally made themselves ugly. This they did so that they would not attract any attention to themselves. It was better one endured in this manner than to fall into the hands of these soldiers who lacked respect for decency, morality, and human life.

At a point, I began to forget what my aunt looked like. She left when I was still asleep and came back when darkness had fallen and supper had since been served.

The 'Atukwa' lamp which provided the light we used in the house was not bright enough to light up the place and people's faces. It could not light up one's face for any proper identification.

So, when she came back in the evening, I did not see her face. I was either too sleepy or the light was not bright enough or both.

Mother encouraged her sister and gave her all the assistance she needed. It later became even clearer that my mother herself came to be also at risk. She deliberately appeared unkempt to make the soldiers believe that she was not that attractive or young.

I was privy to discussions to fade Mum's beauty and make her appear dirty and ugly. She shaved her hair and wore tattered clothes to dispel attraction.

I was however the main source of deterrence as she went everywhere with me to my chagrin. She became a shadow of what she used to be. Perhaps this worked for no one took her away from us in those evil days.

Mum however was just 35 years when the war broke out. She was good-looking and appeared rich as well. She did not frankly look like one who was in a war. She looked well-fed, something suspicious and more like an offence to appear rich and well-fed in those evil days. While she did all within her power to fade her beauty and dim its radiance, it was painful to hear that she was held by her people, and almost killed.

One day, she went to the neighboring village for a visit. This village, Ama-Orie was however under the control of Biafra soldiers. I still do not know why we did not move over to this area, where our soldiers were stationed and occupied. We remained rather in our village with the federal soldiers. I did not understand this even till now. I believed that going to be refugees elsewhere was not attractive at all and besides the federal soldiers were not harming us deeply as much as I knew. So, we chose to visit our relatives in Ama-Orie for we had quite a number of them there and there were other things we had to do over there.

In going to Ama-Orie, one had to cross a big checkpoint at the boundary between our village and Ama-Orie. It was stationed at a place called Ugba Ukwu. It was at this point that the Biafrans stood and mounted a checkpoint. Everyone crossing into Ama-Orie or going out was thoroughly searched and interrogated by Biafran soldiers.

So it was that my mother went to visit in Ama-Orie. As she was coming back, she was stopped at the checkpoint manned by Biafra's soldiers, interrogated, and detained. Her unkempt nature could not deceive the Biafran soldiers into letting her pass without stopping her to interrogate her. They wanted to find out why she was looking well fed when others were looking lean and hungry. The accusations continued as they finally judged her to be a collaborator and a saboteur.

This was the greatest accusation anyone could be labeled with in those days on the Biafra's side. Anyone that had the misfortune of being thus labeled, had a great task clearing or exonerating himself or herself.

Most oftentimes, the ones thus accused don't always escape it. They were either shot summarily or asked to dig their graves. In retrospect, it was like a cancer that ate up the entire efforts of preserving the newfound independence of Biafra.

And so, it was, that my mother painfully and tearfully recounted how she was raising three children without a husband she did not know where he was, if dead or alive. She told them how she too was suffering like any other Biafran and contributing her own quota to the war effort. The soldiers did not believe all she said. It all fell on deaf ears. She was judged, found guilty, and resultantly condemned to death.

She was handed a spade to dig her own grave in the middle of the midday sun. This was the punishment for 'Sabos', the offense my mother allegedly committed. She went about weakly digging what was going to be her final resting place amidst thoughts about what would become of us. As things went on, she went about this morbid activity of scratching the earth to make her grave out of it.

I wondered why you would be asked to dig your own grave. No one had time to waste in digging another's grave. It was the days of hunger and lack. It was better the one that was going to die dug his or her own grave using his or her energy and strength that was not going to be needed again.

It was also to hammer in the severity of your offense to the condemned that as you dug, you would be filled with regret of these actions that have brought you condemnation. People who watched the spectacle were also very petrified and stricken with fear. Therefore, went away from repeating the same errors. So, it was in those and Mum had a taste of it.

It had always been said by men of the old that he who was not carrying anything cannot have something fall off his head to break. So, it was that a man who was my parent's acquaintance was coming along from the neighboring village Ogbe-ke to our village. As he was passing and saw my mother, the miserable and pitiful state she was in, he stopped.

Upon enquiry, my mother recounted what happened. The man bravely took up the matter with the soldiers. He told the soldiers that he would vouch for this woman's integrity. He further told them that she could not do what they were accusing her of. He also told them that he had known my parents over the years, that they were respectable and that mother could not have been a saboteur or fraternized with the enemy as a prostitute as they alleged. To crown it all, he told them he was prepared to die in the place of my mother. This did it. The soldiers looked at themselves and released my mother.

That was how Mother almost lost her life at the hands of her people. It was also how she came back to me particularly as young as I was. I probably needed her more than my older brothers. It could have been unthinkable to lose her at this point in my life. Her return was deeply appreciated. After she recounted her ordeal, she revisited and added to all the measures she had in place to avoid more embarrassments in the future.

Some of the measures she took were to slim down and shave her hair to the skin like one that was bereaved. This last incident greatly dampened her and made her understand in clear terms that in this dispensation, anything could happen. She went deeper into prayers,

> "Hearken unto the voice of my cry,
> My king, and my god
> ..." (Psalm 5)

This was her favorite psalm. While still in bed, I heard her praying with the above psalm. Her solace and protection could only be found in God. She believed in God without doubts or reservations. She prayed like never before and drew very close to God.

Early in the morning she woke up and prayed, reading from the book of Psalms. This added in no small way to ensure mum's religiosity and nearness to God. It was also why kwashiorkor and other adversities of the war did not devastate our family but for Chinwe that was allowed to depart. My two brothers and I did not ever wear the edema boots of Kwashiorkor.

As I turned sleepily in the morning, I heard her praying, calling upon God to lead us, guide us, and protect us all along the way. Sometimes she woke us up and we joined her to pray.

Praying became a routine we were used to during the war. Mum was a practicing catholic and her reverence to the mother of Jesus Christ was unrivalled. We shared in her devotions naturally. This formed the basis and the bedrock of our lives as Christians even later in our lives. Our survival therefore in the war could not be attributed to any other reason than that that was hinged on God and mum's prayers.

Mum was a very religious person as has been said. She went to school in a catholic convent in the late 1940s. She wanted to become a Rev. Sister but life and her schedule had other plans for her. The school she attended was in Eme-kuku. Eme-kuku is situated in Owerri North LGA of Imo state.

She sacrificed greatly for the education she acquired then. It was something I greatly pondered when she told me that she used to wake up by 4 a.m. every day to go from her father's house in Owerri to Eme-kuku, a distance of about 11 kilometers.

All this sacrifice she made for her early education and the foundation upon which it was laid was Christianity. This thereby impacted highly upon her life and ensured this level of relationship with God in the war.

So, the war situation was a big challenge to her and naturally called up her trust and dependance in God.

As a revised measure, to avoid what happened before, my elder brother joined our company to prove her claims of having gone far deep into motherhood. This measure looked more convincing. She therefore went about with us anywhere she wanted to go. It was convincing to show that you had a child but it was more convincing to prove this beyond any form of doubt when you had two children and they followed you about everywhere.

This was what Mum did and the three of us were regularly seen as we went wherever she went. It cut our own time so short that we hated the very idea of having to move around with her wherever she went. Every woman therefore in the siege was like mum. They were looked upon by the federal soldiers like those to be picked up like a fruit, licked and thrown away again.

It was a pity what women and children suffered. The women, other than mum went about dirty and disheveled just to look unattractive. This was a forgone conclusion of those days. This was a kind of protection they all wore against the randy federal soldiers who would stop at nothing to seize a woman who faintly caught their fancy.

We as children, therefore, cursed the reason why the war came, that we had to go about with our mothers again not as dependants but as defenders to save them from their infernal sex predators.

CHAPTER 5

ADAKU FRANK

There was a woman in our village in those days who became prominent for what she did for us. She was called Adaku Frank. She was from one of the kindreds in our village called Ebi-koro. With the outbreak of hostilities and an eventual shooting war, our brethren came back from far and near to their respective villages. It also included people from our small sleepy village.

Some that came back from Lagos and Kano could speak Hausa and Yoruba fluently. They possessed competence in either Hausa or Yoruba languages or both.

Adaku was in this category. She was fluent in Yoruba and Hausa. She stayed in Lagos for a long time and had a stint in Kano too. When the conflict started, like others she found her way home, the place of her nativity.

She was an amiable person. This quality of hers endeared her to a lot of people even our enemies as events would show. She was however fat and fair and was in her early 40's during the war. She had a certain control over the federal soldiers which could not be physically explained. This she probably did because of her competence in both Yoruba and Hausa languages and her very obvious amiability.

She was fair, plump, and could pass as being beautiful. She was not any man's wife. I did not see any man that she was affiliated with. So, she was free and did what she did without much hindrance.

It was not readily known how she got and wielded this great

influence on the federal soldiers. You would recall that upon a bright and sunny day, our village was sacked by the federal army. While some ran away to the forest as we did, some stayed back and stayed with the occupation force.

So, while we were in the forest, someone had taken control of the situation at home. This was in the form of reining in the federal soldiers. They were to a great extent controlled by Adaku Frank. When they came in the morning, they went straight to her house. It was from here they were dispersed to different locations of the village.

Her father was called Amadi. He was a train driver. My father always referred to him as "engine driver." He was killed in the pogrom of 1966. He built one of the biggest houses in our village. The house was of imperial proportions and outlook. It was positioned by the western approach to our village in the kindred called Ebi-koro.

It was from here that Adaku Frank held sway. I did not also know how 'Frank' got suffixed to her name. This further mystified her personality.

The federal soldiers came to her first in her father's "imperial palace" to receive handouts and instructions on ethics and codes of conduct on how to deal with the villagers. The officers stayed with her in the "palace" while the rest roamed freely in the village to look for spoil.

Cases however that concerned the soldiers were promptly reported to her. She presided over the situation in the whole community in this imperial place. She held and maintained the relationship between the soldiers and the villagers. She ensured that tempers did not boil over. It was so effective that any soldier caught in any misdemeanor was reported to her.

When the information reached her, she quickly arrived at the scene of the event with the air of an imperial majesty, the officers followed behind dutifully. The situation was remedied immediately.

The erring federal soldiers were dragged away immediately. It was so confusing. I was no longer sure who was the captor or the captive. If my cousin had alerted Adaku Frank on time, his fowl would not have probably been killed.

Such cases as taking women forcibly were reported to her. Like a prey in the grips of the terrible, Adaku Frank always intervened and rescued, it was unbelievably magical and incredulous.

I was greatly confounded by the roles Adaku Frank played. From my position, it seemed she knew all these federal soldiers and thus she was able to wield this level of influence and control over them.

Some other villagers were equally confounded by her total control of the situation. It was beyond speculation what she did and how she was this powerful with them. The people could not come to any convincing conclusion that could explain this situation that played out before us. We resigned ourselves to fate and savored this situation as it lasted.

I considered her a "saboteur" because right before the eyes of the villagers, she was freely mixing and parleying with them.

The results of this kind of collaboration were however very obvious to accuse her of such. The general opinion was however that God used her to take harm and molestation away from us. All through the war, she acted like a check ensuring that we were not pushed too hard. She was always seen in the company of these soldiers. They looked very much like her bodyguards surprisingly.

It was however reassuring that one of us was controlling the enemy or so we thought. She was liked, perhaps loved by a lot of people, even the federal soldiers. They called her 'Area madam.'

In these days of uncertainty, a lot has happened and more were threatening to happen. No one seemed to have control of anything. No one also could offer any meaningful explanation of what was going on.

The news had since reached us that Biafra had lost more than half of her territory and Owerri was being threatened again. It was 1969. As at the last count Enugu, Onitsha, and Nsukka had since fallen into federal hands and control. News reached us that Ojukwu had moved his headquarters to Umuahia.

Voice of Biafra was still reeling out news of exploits and Biafra's invincibility. The reassurances and claims had no real basis in reality because they could not be matched by what we saw and heard.

From our place, there was a loud sound of guns that sounded like they were coming from next door. It was also told us the sounds were coming from a gun testing site at Ohuba. This is a suburban town of old Owerri province in the present-day Imo state.

One thing we did not have a total grasp of was information. The source of information could not be relied upon.

We heard a lot of things that we could not in any way verify or validate independently or otherwise. It could be said that there was a torrent of information that reached us which we sieved just to know which was true and which was not. It did not matter how much of the information we processed; we usually came to wrong conclusions as events eventually played out and contradicted them.

It was all part of the situation we found ourselves. The Ohuba testing site came as the other piece of information. Part of the confusion also came from the fact that when guns were fired, it was not known who fired it. In our case, we believed that every gunshot we heard was fired by our troops. It buoyed us greatly and gave us lots of false hope.

There was always this debate that the sound of the guns were the guns of our boys and that we were dealing a great and deadly blow on the enemy.

We were in the grips of patriotism and were blinded by it. Everyone wanted us to win the war and have the right to self-determination.

After all we have been through in the larger federation; it was only fair we came out of the conflict tops. A defeat was unthinkable and unfair. We had lost our brothers and sisters, fathers and mothers to death in macabre and gruesome circumstances. Their blood cried respectively from the different parts of the country. Who was going to pacify the blood that was spilled and cried for vengeance, who was going to quench our thirst for justice or avenge the death of our kith and kin?

We have been pursued down to our homestead like slaves and common criminals, with the hatchet raised and about to fall upon our shaved skulls and distended bellies. What was our offense? We had nowhere else to go but to fight or wait for an eventual death from the barrels of their unthinking guns.

From what I beheld; we were too fired up by an unrivaled love of our fatherland to accept a defeat or even walk towards it. So, feats that the enemy achieved were appropriated to us. That was why every gun that boomed or sounded in the distance was deemed to have come from the guns and barrels of our soldiers. Though news about one or two acts of gallantry filtered in, assured, assuaged, and watered our perched hearts with precious hope of reassurances.

Furthermore, it firmed up our belief and strengthened it that victory was surely ours despite having lost two-thirds of the land mass that was Biafra. Our faith was however kept alive by the seeming invincibility of our army as the news reached us rightly or wrongly but most usually wrongly. The propaganda machinery was well-oiled and was reeling out stories of victory upon baseless claims.

As a child, I never believed that we were going to lose the war. Most people could not bring themselves to agree that it was not going to favour us also. As a child, we were made aware of the war and its execution, its failings and successes, were reeled out to all and sundry. So, it was not strange to us what the news was all about and what our expectations were. This primarily was based upon what I heard the elders say.

Our drooping spirits were yet strengthened by stories of superhuman or extraordinary gallantry of our men. Such accounts as that of Osuji Steve, (23rd October 2012) and Wikipedia of what happened at Abagana on the 31st March 1968 quickly reached us and circulated everywhere like wildfire in the dry season.

The news acted like an elixir to our spirits that had started drooping and failing. It revived the hearers and assured us that victory was surely coming and was really around the corner, our faith in our abilities being justified.

One of such other exploits was told of a rampaging Saracen that had broken through the Biafran defenses and was heading straight to our forces. The last bazookas having been fired, and other efforts to stop it having also failed, left the men with no remedy other than an imminent and violent death.

As the armored personnel carrier came on advancing, spraying bullets, cutting down leaves and tree branches and of course human lives. A Biafran soldier braced all odds, came out of hiding, his action bolt rifle in hand, cocked it, and put a pinch of sand in the nuzzle not before he circled the sand three times around it.

After this, the story had it that the gallant man hit the butt of his rifle on the earth with minimal force, raised it, took aim, and fired at the oncoming Saracen. This stopped it dead in its tracks, demobilized and dismembered as the bullet hit what seemed like its armory.

The jubilation of the Biafran platoon was unprecedented even though they would have loved to have the Saracen intact for later use. At this brazenness, the federal soldiers took to their heels just like the felling of Goliath by David and the resultant chaos in the camp of the Philistines.

Such stories whether they happened or not sparked off fresh fires of patriotism and pride that burnt for a while, sustained our ego and hope in the ongoing war that we would surely win it. Such stories thrilled everyone including me and made me wish I was on the war front and defending my father's land, Biafra, and her course. But I was just 7 years old.

Our pride and invincibility as a nation were awoken by news of such gallantry. Even after the war, when it was obvious that it was over, we were still expecting a turning point, a certain 'Deus ex Machina' to come about in our overall favour, somehow to prove the stuff we were made of.

Osere

This was a phenomenon that played out in those days which as a child confounded me. I did not come to terms with what it was or what to make out of it.

On a fine cloudless day, with the sun high above the sky. The birds chirped excitedly. The breeze blew gently too and brought to our ears with it the sound and echoes of distant guns that reminded us that the war was still going on. The federal troops had gone and left us alone. The exigencies of war had forced them out from Owerri for it was recaptured by Biafra in 1968 which was held for a long time.

And so, it was that my attention was drawn to the commotion that was on the road that passes through our village to the next village Okolochi. I ran out to see what was amiss. Experience had shown in the course of the war that any delay at such times might mean death or some terrible situations. It was one lesson we had collectively learned. So, as I came out to see the reason for the commotion, I saw a sight that I still recall even as I write. It was a row of wounded and disabled men who limped along the road to a destination none could immediately determine.

Some were being carried in raffia beds while others were simply limping along with sticks as crutches. Many had bandages on their heads, hands, and legs. Some behaved like they were crazy. No one knew who they were or where they were going or coming from. As I beheld, I wondered what could have made these move from where they were staying to a new place. Because of their disabilities which had also affected the way they moved; they were called 'osere'.

It was later learnt that the osere's movement was an evacuation of wounded soldiers. When a town was threatened by federal forces, the frail and the wounded of the Biafran side in the town were moved out first to avoid being unable to be attended to when the invasion started.

As we found out, whenever they passed our village, it became common knowledge that we were at risk too, and started getting ready to move because an invasion was imminent.

CHAPTER 6

EVENTS MARKING THOSE DAYS

The pain, hopelessness, and confusion deepened in those days. The days and events further went deeper into more madness and made us gaze with utter amazement. The walking strides on the road became longer and faster least one was caught at the wrong place by the more consistent air raids of the federal air force planes. The days became longer and pregnant with uncertainty as the nights became shorter without answers to the ensuing confusion.

The events of the day had become our undoing by default. They filled us with trepidation, for sunlight and fair weather exposed us to persistent air raids. Sunshine which was as good as fair weather was dreaded because of the foregoing.

We noticed that air raids were more in clearer skies. As soon as the sun rose high enough, the roar of jet engines filled us with fear and dread. The onset of sunlight typified it.

So, on the days when the sun came up and the skies were devoid of thick cumulonimbus, our hearts skipped a lot of beats because the roar of jet engines would come that filled us with raw terror. Who knew if this coming was going to be it and end it all for us? This was our thoughts. It was full of fear and uncertainty.

It kept us running even into the rough embrace of the forest. It was a terrible way to leave. One was not sure of the next minute of his life, if tomorrow would ever come or not if the sun would be seen rising out of her home or not. It was a morbid situation that defied our input towards any solution and elimination of the problem.

This therefore constrained people to be walking under trees. Buildings with zinc roofing were avoided and shaded with palm fronds. There were not many such roofs with zinc roofs around our place. The majority of the roofs were thatched and posed no much threat. However, the zinc roofs attracted attention and were targeted. They reflected sunlight and were more visible from the air than their thatched equivalent, or so we thought. It was believed to be a training facility for soldiers or had one thing or the other to do with the prosecution of the war which must be destroyed.

All such roofs in the village were therefore covered with palm fronds to obscure their reflexive ability. Because of the increased air raids, most activities ceased after ten o clock till late in the evening, for fear of one being caught unawares where one could not quickly take cover.

Even attempts at continuing our education that stopped at the outset of the conflict were also scuttled by the persistent air raids. When we woke up in the morning and bathed, we went to school.

Our school was temporarily situated at the Catholic mission in the village called Ogige Okwu. The roof of the church building was covered with palm fronds to dull its reflective ability and make it invisible from the air. We started school early in this place. The church hall was demarcated with plywood to divide or delineate the different classes.

So, in the morning we left for school. It was rather earlier than normal so that we would close before the sun came, before any air raid commenced.

The school closed before 11 a.m. The school hours were so short that we were roundly called 'Nde ri efeoku'. This meant that our meals did not get cold before we got back. It was a funny spectacle to behold as we came back from school almost immediately we left home.

It was unthinkable to be in school when the fighter planes came on the scene. It seemed that this must be the end for the one because of the randomness by which death came from the air, no one knew whose turn was next. It was a morbid way of living. The church that was converted to a school was still visible even with the palm fronds that tried without much success to cover it.

As small children and pupils, we walked to the catholic mission called Ogige Okwu and learned what our teacher whom we called 'Nna anyi ukwu Eke' had to teach us. He was the only teacher for the entire primary one.

He taught and related with us in a very high-handed manner. He blended so much into the situation then, that of fear and uncertainty about our overall lives. He was a bullish man who found it very hard to laugh. I did not know if his inability to articulate a smile or laughter was because of the war or his overall nature. Whichever it was, Nna Ukwu Eke was always melancholic. We dreaded him and kept away from annoying him lest he descended on us with fury that made us cry and not desirous of coming to school again.

Our lives suffered in all ramifications. The enlightenment brought by education for our minds was effectively stopped. The air raids and those behind them were responsible for it.

We stopped going to school altogether when Ogige Okwu was targeted and the bomb fell nearby around my father's hut. The risk became too much and the school closed down. So, the three years of the conflict saw us without going to school or any attempt at formal education.

As those days lasted, our family went back again to Okwuotamiri to seek refuge. We always preferred taking cover in this forest or going there to hide because it was very dense. It afforded us cover no other place could. It did not matter what dangers wild animals posed. We felt it was safer therein and could effectively handle the threat of animals.

It was therefore like looking for a pin in a haystack to see anyone therein from the air. We were therefore very relaxed in the bowels of this forest; we always preferred it to other places that were not dense as this place was.

There were no bomb shelters. There were also no basements to run into during air raids. Our only chance of escape was the forest. And so, it was that mum always prepared food we carried to the forest which had become our bomb shelter. It was enough for all of us or close to it.

With what we had, we left for the forest that was a kilometer and a half away. We came back in the evening when it was safe to return when the sun had gone down in the horizon.

The forest indeed offered us shelter and protection. We utilized this opportunity offered by the wild and dangerous forest to shelter in them as the days came. We left in the morning before 10 o'clock.

While in the forest, we ate the meals we came with at the appropriate time. We as children ran off, went about, and rummaged in the thick forest looking for fun and berries.

We occasionally picked berries and licked them while we waited for sunset to come. Such berries we referred to as 'Ubene' were more available. We met them always and licked until our tongues and the roof of our mouths even our hard palates blistered.

'Utu' was very rare and it was great luck to see it. Our faces lighted up with excitement when it was sighted. We plucked it. It used to slap our cheeks even when ripe but we did not mind. It served other purposes for us because we used the housing as 'Apa'. This was a small vessel we put our shares of fish from our soup and kept them by the fireplace.

So, the utu was treasured. Other ones like velvet tamarind 'Nchichi' were common but it was not the season in those days of our flight to the forest.

These we did and waited for the sun to go down in the evening. We did not make noise lest we attract attention both from the air and around us, or so we thought.

Thank God for the weather. Our flight was usually in the dry season or immediately after the season preceding it. There were instances of snake bites but were not to epidemic proportions. We did not need to erect shelters. We stayed under thick foliage and were sheltered from the sun. Mum carried a mat she used to lie down on the rough forest floor and waited for the sun's going down.

Even nature provided water for us in the forest. 'Uju' was the name given to water that percolated at the base of a shrub that had a vessel-like shape. While we rummaged about in the forest, we met and drank the cold fresh water of the uju that got there by rain.

And so, while we rummaged, I had to be particularly careful of 'Obere ogbuo'. This was an insect that suddenly perched or rather jumped on you in their numbers and bit you when you strayed into their territory, thus the name 'Obere ogbuo'.

They jumped on me once and bit me mercilessly. I was deeply worried about this insect. Their abode was cleverly camouflaged as folded leaves held together to avoid detection. It was painful enough to have left civilization to come to the forest but more painful to be bitten by Obere ogbuo.

I avoided trees that had soldier ants too because they guarded their colony ferociously just like we were guarding our territory from the federal troops. I watched the ants as they stood guard and bared their teeth warning any invader to stay away.

I hid their warning and stayed away. I watched as they moved about the length and breadth of the stem of the little shrub I was about to climb angrily expecting to see and deal with any intruder.

I climbed a shrub once and failed to notice their presence. I paid dearly for my oversight. The ants launched at me with a rage. Before I knew it, they were all over me and bit me with all their strength. We called them 'Nfu'.

So, as we found ourselves in the forest and I stood in front of a tree and contemplated climbing, I was very careful to know which one had 'Nfu'and which was free of it. 'Evu', (the hornet) was even more painful when it stung you. A story had it of one boy who was stung by a hornet, his tongue got elongated three times its original length and the boy had to carry his tongue with his bare hands. It made scary but interesting stories.

Because of where we were living, a place bounded on all sides by the forest, such stories were rife. But we were fairly new in these parts. Our hurried introduction to these parts was because of the war. We had lived all our short lives as kids in the townships at Onitsha where my father worked as a roadman. But at the threat to the town, we ran to our village in the southeast of Nigeria called Amaeze- Obibi Ezena.

So, stories about hornets and other things we encountered in the forest really scared me and I was fast learning and also paying dearly for the lessons and experiences.

That was how I became very careful about wasps and hornets. In my estimations, I thought it made one lose consciousness. I thought of the much it could do in harming people because of what I saw and heard it did to people.

I wondered what they guarded so dutifully in their colony that made them defend it with all their strength. I dreaded them and looked carefully before I climbed any tree in search of berries. I also told myself that these stories were better heard than experienced.

Once or twice snakes met people on trees, pursued and dealt deadly blows on them as in biting. Such unfortunate people ended up dying or were subjected to terrible traditional Medicare as 'inu udu'. This was a procedure of treatment which consisted of concoctions of different substances. The person was made to drink to expel or neutralize the poison that got into him with the snake's bite.

Whichever way it was, it was a painful procedure; the bite or the cure. I was so scared about this that in addition to checking to find the aforementioned, I took particular interest in making sure that a cobra, we called (echu) was not on the prowl before climbing.

I could not imagine what happened when a viper or cobra met one on a tree or anywhere else. The very thought of it sent shivers down my spine.

Even as we traced our way to the forest to take cover from air raids, both sides of the pathway were covered by forest. So, the dove, we called 'ovu' always cooed on either side of the pathway. Our people were superstitious. It spanned across all areas of our life. Superstition about birds and other things revolved around our existence as a people.

The dove was superstitiously regarded as one that told when something was going to be wrong or right. She was considered a harbinger of both good and bad tidings. It cooed to warn of an impending doom or of good tidings that was in the future.

It was like the owl we called 'ikwikwi'that hooted in the night. This was associated with the death of a family or member of the kindred and the resultant passage of such souls to the land of the dead.

The owl was therefore regarded as a harbinger of bad tidings that told us when one was going to die. At such times, she hooted ominously and persistently nearby.

The dove however played a double role. If as we went to take cover, the dove cooed loudly on the left side of the path, it was interpreted as a bad sign or omen.

Mum and other elderly people quickly intoned, 'ovu vuru ihe ovu ahia azuru la ya' (let the dove carry all her wares away, it will have no chance to sell, and no one will patronize her) this was a rebuttal or an antidote against the impending catastrophe that the dove allegedly warned. It was usually cancelled as the people believed the above rebuttal.

It was still a point to ponder. I ruminated upon why the dove cooed on the left to alert them of an impending danger like she was privy. And a reasonable number of times, it played out as alleged among the people, which was why they believed and listened for the cooing of the dove.

And so, on this bright sunny day, as we walked wearily to the forest, the dove was far away in the forest and cooed on our left. It made all the elderly ones uneasy. It seemed like it was warning of an impending doom for indeed something very terrible happened that day.

As we prepared as usual to leave for our air raid shelter at Okwuotamiri forest, Mum ensured we did what had to be done which had become our routine. We packed our things and all we needed.

On this day too, my elder brother, Chika tried to get out of the line and out of Mum's control. He said that he was not going to take cover that day. He saw our peers lazing around and playing while we had packed to go away to the forest, a very boring thing we abhorred.

Mum turned and looked sternly at him. No one told him to get back in line for Okwuotamiri. As we entered the pathway to the place, Chika could not understand why we could be wasting precious time going to the forest for protection from the sun up till the going down of the same. Mum scolded him and refused to let him stay back in the village for anything in the world.

One of our cousins who was called Uche worsened matters for us. He followed us as we went along laughing and taunting us. He referred to us as spineless men who ran away to take cover in the forest with women.

He was loquacious and always wanted to be heard in every matter. We played together a lot in the sand at the 'ama' before the war reached our village. We had variously shared thoughts of what life had in store for us; what we would love to grow up to be. Also, we had set up mock families together and chosen wives out of our sisters and cousins in this mock family setup that we saw our mothers and fathers do.

It was therefore in this manner that Uche ran after us and taunted us sour, laughed loudly at our cowardice by running away to take cover in the bowels of the forest. He further said that if we were men like him, we should stay at home and man the home front like him rather than running away like women and girls. Our mother's presence made us utter no word in reply to Uche's words and insults.

Chika my elder brother was swayed by this taunting from Uche and as such was bent on staying back at home. But Mum could not take any of Chika's dissension. Her cold stare at Chika and by extension all of us made us continue on the way towards safety without looking back again at Uche.

As we left the village and got on the path to the forest, Uche still ran after us and pelted us with his words. Finally, he dropped back as we got on the path to Okwuotamiri, some reasonable distance from home.

We concentrated on the immediate task of getting to the forest and contending with the numerous doves that cooed and rebutting their evil tidings which they filled the atmosphere with. We became less concerned with Uche and his empty words. We plodded on and forgot what was behind in the village.

At Okwuotamiri, some settled down to nap while my brother Chika and I went in search of rodents and wild berries we called 'Ubene'. And soon we settled down too to the serenity of the forest with intermittent clatter of birds. The singing of birds and their chirpings filled the air and naturally marked the fact that we were in the kingdom of animals.

We felt at home in the forest and safe surprisingly. It gave us an unrivaled sense of security that we could not get anywhere else during the war. It was the singular reason why we always ran to this place to hide from the planes that struck terror in our agitated and fearful hearts. We felt quite safe and were only able to rest for a while in the bowels of the Okwuotamiri forest.

We were not so much as worried about the other dangers of the forest like wild animals as has been said. Even though we had no insurance against them, we were nonetheless rest assured that it was not as bad as the air raids that killed us without a second thought or chance to defend ourselves.

It also afforded us time to think and probably pray for ourselves in the ensuing madness that had engulfed us like a conflagration.

The forest was therefore one place we could run to and for as long as we were there, we thought more clearly about our lives and focused on how and where best our whole lot fell.

So, on this particular day as soon as we settled down, some dozed off, while others were alert. We were not the only ones. Other friendly families came to take shelter too. So, did it happen that there was a frightening roar of an airplane that was almost flying at the level of the shrub we were contemplating climbing. We ducked unconsciously like we did not want the people on the plane to see us. We dived deeper into the foliage to hide from the plane that had just flown past.

The next moment there was a loud explosion that shook the ground we stood. We ran to where Mum was out of sheer fright. She was also awoken by the heavy roar of a plane that just flew by. She instinctively looked at the three of us huddled together in great fear near her.

The look on Mum's face was like 'Did I not tell you that it was going to happen'. It was like a confirmation of why she had insisted we come to the forest to take cover.

Her intuition was always accurate and never came to failing. Mum's intuition was very accurate. She was like having the fact that something was wrong and that whatever it was, was not going to catch us on the wrong side. So, her looking our way was like a confirmation of her role as one who was responsible for bringing us up. She opined that her authority and demands on us should not in any way be questioned. It was confirmed in very clear terms. It was like scales fell off our eyes as we stared bleary-eyed at her as the echo of the bomb faded in the distance.

Our flight was justified and Mum's sternness in these matters justified. Chika's opposition melted further with the loud explosion that had come from the village we left a while ago. He stood deflated and stared back at Mum with a subdued admission of guilt. Mbanugo had not raised any opposition and had not given Mum any problems at all. He stood too and watched Mum to see what she would do next. We were so tied to her and were very willing to listen and obey her every command. The three of us stood like the musketeers before her and awaited further directives of what to do from our dear mother.

And so, it was that a lot raced through our minds. Who knew where the bomb had fallen? That the bomb fell in the village we left a few minutes ago was not a matter to be debated but the question should be on whose house did it fall, and who and who were wounded or even died. These were the collective worries of all of us.

But mum worried most. She knew more than all of us. Dad had come to visit a day earlier after a long time. He was not able to come to see us. He was in the service of Biafra's civil service. He did not follow when we ran to the forest. He was not always with us. He was not always available.

Even when we ran from Onitsha, he came home briefly and left again. He was always on the move to contribute to the war effort. But on this particular day, he came to visit after a long while.

Upon all these considerations, our stay in the forest became indeed a long uncomfortable one. Mum's mood affected us. When she was happy, we were happy and when moody, it affected our overall moods too.

As she sat and went into a deep reverie, we stole glances at her even from where we went to catch on with our trifles. Mum at a point paced about waited for the sun to go down.

We could not even contemplate going back to the village immediately. It was not evening yet, for we feared that the plane could come back. So, we stayed put in the bowels of the forest and waited impatiently for the sun to go down.

But as we waited for the going down of the sun, the wind suddenly stopped blowing- the leaves became still and stopped being ruffled. There was an unusual quietness as the numerous birds that clattered stopped their very noisy cacophony.

It seemed as if creation and nature commiserated with us and shared our apprehension. This however heightened our sense of foreboding. It seemed like nature watched us, their gaze poured all over us, and their pity at what news awaited us at home. It was all moodiness within and around us. It was certain that something had happened at home. The sign was all over the air in one show of pathetic fallacy.

We could not fully wait for the going down of the sun. We could not wait anymore in the forest as our apprehension grew in leaps and bounds.

When it was like 4 pm, Mum said that we should go. We packed up and headed home. She could not bear the thought of staying out any further from whatever that had happened. The bomb and its effects were a serious cause of concern for her.

We packed up and trudged home in great uncertainty at what happened at home, surely and consistently our steps brought us closer home to ground zero.

There was so much commotion that no one even knew we had come home as used to be the case. Confusion had taken over and reigned without any challenge. This was even as the bomb was dropped about four hours earlier, it seemed it just happened. People were still milling around with their hands on their cheeks and in great sorrow. Some were still crying and shaking their heads in a real show of emotions at what happened and the situation we have inextricably found ourselves in as a people.

The cry was more like when would all this madness stop? When would our blood stop flowing and the death of our loved ones cease to make us sigh and cry? When would the destruction of what is left of us as a people come to an end? No one seemed to have the answer to these questions. But all looked up to providence and depended on the pendant machinations.

Some however discussed in low and sorrowful tones, talked about what had happened while some walked briskly about, clearing the debris and still helping the wounded. Survivors were also being pulled out of the rubble. It was a bloody day in the Onye-neke's family.

In all eleven people died and that sadly included Uche who taunted us earlier as we went to take shelter. While he was laughing and jeering at us that morning full of life, he did not know it was going to be his last day on earth.

And like our mother said, Uche was looking for companions to the underworld. No wonder his persuasions earlier that morning. But it did not make much meaning to me.

Uche was a friend but his badly mangled body lay forlornly on the ground somewhere for something he did not know about. There were many like him whose lives ended abruptly, their future and destiny thrown away in the ocean of foolishness that can never be retrieved.

In my mind, it made a great impression about how visionary mothers could be. Uche's house took a direct hit from the bomb. It fell on the back wall of their house. Their house was badly damaged. They were inside at the time. His mother and sister died in the bomb incident too.

When we got into my father's house, Dad had just come back from ground zero. Though he had not come back to the house, the news of his safety had reached Mum when we came into the village. She was finally reassured that nothing had happened to our father.

When we came into the house, we saw him physically. I also discovered that without being told, Mum loved Dad very much. Her fretting about his overall safety in the incident drove the point home. His being around was very necessary to Mum's overall goodness. So, as we got home and Dad appeared without any wound or a scratch, Mother was highly elated. Though she did not show it openly, her general disposition was the voice that said it.

We had been spared again from harm. We had come very close to being touched by this senseless war and providently escaped. It was a source of great sorrow and pity for those who had to die, those whose loved ones died without a farewell at least. It was like that in this senselessness.

One was alive in the morning and gone by midday. A whole family was broken into pieces before sunset. Friends parted not because they wanted to but because they had been forced to be separated by death which was not brought by natural circumstances but some senselessness that has continued to defy and reject reason. The wailing and loud lamentation in those families did not cease for a time.

However, we picked up the bits and pieces of our lives again and moved on. Somewhere at the back of our minds, we waited for our turn. It was wishful thinking that we could not be killed too for as this senselessness continued; it was sure to come. Those who died in the incident were even envied. They had died and knew no more sorrows, had lost all apprehensiveness of what was going to happen or otherwise. The very thought of this was killing in its own right. I heard Mum discussing with her fellows that it was better to die than live in the horrors of what threatened you daily. They envied those who died.

They knew no more sorrows nor worried about where to run to or concerned about how to fight kwashiorkor. It was like an obsession that made the rounds. The apprehension of what was going to happen next was enough to crack someone open. It was undesirable to be found in such a state of not knowing if the sun would surely rise again when tomorrow comes with you witnessing it.

Dad narrated what happened while he was around. He was drinking palm wine with my cousin's husband who was a captain in the Biafran army. He was called Dyke. He was a handsome and clever man. I liked his appearance as a Biafran soldier. He came with a thickly starched uniform and a backsman. It gave me a good impression that the Biafran army was indeed close to being a professional outfit based on what I saw in Dyke.

And so, it was that while Dad was drinking with this man, they had the distant sound of the plane that got louder and louder by the second. Eventually, it whooped past over the hut that was my father's. In the difference of half a second the explosion that did the damage came on.

Dad said that the impact of the explosion that did so much damage and killed eleven people including my cousin Uche was inexplicable.

The cup of palm wine in his hand was literary taken from him and dropped back on the table before them. Dyke quickly got up and came to my father's aid being an accomplished soldier and used to explosions. "Sorry sir." He quickly said.

Debris as soot fell from the thatched roof of our hut and into the glasses of palm wine of both men. He further said that immediately screams from the Onye-nekes family rent the midmorning tedium. People started shouting for help. Those who got wounded and realized their misfortune started crying and wailing. Dad and dyke immediately left for the ground zero.

At the gate to their compound, he saw a man who was wounded and lay on the ground unmoving. He weakly called out to Dad for help, "Nda Adol. Please don't let me die here." His name was Jonas. Dad quickly commanded help for him. So, both of them helped a lot of other people who were in one wounded state or the other.

The dead were pulled out of the rubble and the wounded were attended to in the best way possible because there was no Medicare for such extensive wounds. The best Medicare they got was the expression of pity and its resultant vocalization in the form of "ndo nu" (sorry) It was a very pitiful sight.

My cousin Christopher was lying down in his father's hut when the explosion occurred. He was having malaria and could not go to the forest to check on his traps or anywhere else. And so, as the bomb fell, he heard a thud of a sound at his head. He looked to see that it was shrapnel from the bomb that had just fallen. He immediately got up and went to Onye-nekes family to help in the rescue effort. It was indeed very bad for the Onye-nekes family and all of us. It served to remind us that we were not spared. If the bomb could locate our kindred and cause this much damage, it was only a matter of time before the rest of us were cut down too.

The senselessness of the war could not be overemphasized. In all eleven people lost their lives in just a moment for something they did not know nor contributed to its being in place.

Our lives consisted of these events in the war. One was alive in the morning and before the evening was dead not of natural causes but death of a violent nature. Our lives were likened to that of the civet that we hunted for meat in those days. If the bush rat missed her path, she was caught easily. So it was that when one was found in a place that he should not be found, it gave room for troubles and misfortunes.

I was sobered up by the death of Uche. I just could not bring myself to believe that he died. Mother was devastated too because of the death of her friends including Uche's mother. Some other friends of hers that died pained her very much.

It buttressed the point that it was only providence that could guarantee escape from death and such misfortunes that were fatal and confronted us daily in the war.

And so, our sheltering in the forest naturally assumed a more serious dimension. Before 9 a.m., we were gone to the place of shelter in the middle of the forest at Okwuotamiri.

This period was the time of the great battles to recapture Owerri by Biafra. There were therefore lots of activities by the federal army to overturn Owerri's victory.

Dad moved back to his station. The times were difficult ones; movement was made almost impossible by the war. Dad however came with the help of people who led them through safe paths with a rare form of clairvoyance.

We went back to the same boring routine that had been in place before now. It was not boring because there was a lot of apprehension about the war that was raging in one or two approaches to Owerri.

Air raids were incessant and we took no chances. Uche's death had dealt a big blow to my psyche and it made me obey Mum in all she told me and not only me but my two brothers also.

The bomb incident reinforced the importance of going to take shelter after all. Those who were not going before started going. The forest became a beehive of activities as more people came to take cover as the morning came and the sun came out. It became an important aspect of our lives that was no longer ignored or taken lightly. It was usually said that 'Osondu agwu ike', which translates to mean that 'one does not get tired running to save his life'

A day came when we did not go to take cover. It was harvesting season and some corns were harvested. And so, it was that I was roasting corn in the compound after our home.

This family where I roasted the corn always had a fire in their 'obi'. It was the type that was ideal for roasting corn. As I was roasting the corn, the sound of a plane came on. The sound could be heard as it approached us.

Everywhere resultantly became quiet. People took cover as best as they could. It was just like when a kite came on the scene and chicks had to run to take cover and hide.

So, it was with us. But I could not run to take cover. In addition to the fact that I would be exposed, I did not want my corn to burn in the fire. It seemed I was the only one in the whole world. The place was quieter than a graveyard. There was not a single soul anywhere.

It was so quiet that we thought that keeping quiet would make the plane assume there were no people around to attack or that the plane and her handlers had come down to our homesteads and were moving from one house to another to choose which house to enter by the noise therein. It was a great delusion that pervaded.

I could not run away to the house to hide because of the considerations above. I had this sick feeling that the plane was going to spot me if I made any move. So, I sat still and tended my corn as it popped in the fire. As everywhere became quiet, the only sound that came and kind of filled the place was the sound of my corn popping in the fire. The popping was so loud amid grave silence. It even had some orchestration as if directed at what was happening in the interim; the plane.

However, in my mind, I directed the popping sound at the plane as my anti-aircraft gun. I wished that the mere popping of my corn brought down the plane that had struck so much terror upon our people.

My corn continued popping; my fear and apprehension turned into excitement that I had confronted the enemy bold-faced when everyone else went to hide. The plane circled the area and left and did not drop any bombs.

My corn got roasted and I got back home with a smile of satisfaction around my lips while others were crawling out of hiding with their hearts pushing up their ribs. I beat my chest that I had contributed to the cause of Biafra even with my corn and when it mattered most as others ducked.

The last bomb that fell in our kindred had taught us very bitter lessons about how not to toy with the war and its abilities to kill and maim.

If childhood fantasies could count and turn the tide in the favour of a people, mine would have surely counted. But what we were contending with was more than mere fantasy. It was an orchestration that was targeted at killing people, maiming, and destroying properties. It was not at my level but at the level of reasons that we did not adduce nor were called to offer any opinions. Yet we fell victim to the evil we were not part of, children and adults alike.

CHAPTER 7

THE 'JIGA' MENACE (AKWA NTUGBU)

As the war progressed, we were afflicted with lots of strange sicknesses with manifestations of a very bizarre nature. These marked our lives and unleashed untold pain and misery.

'Akwa ntugbu' or jiga was a very strange one indeed. It could be said with certainty that after the war, I have not seen one that was afflicted by this. It was very surprising to me to see people's toes perforated by a white roundish organism which we generally referred to as "jiga."

It grew to a size of a small pebble in the toe of its victim. As it entered your toes, it increased in stature. It drew nourishment from its host and therefore grew. You knew you had it when your toe where it had taken refuge started itching at a point.

And so, it was that I had such an itching on my left middle toe. I promptly suspected Jiga because it was prevalent. I went to one of my cousins who had become an expert 'surgeon' in jiga extraction.

This art my cousin acquired in jiga extraction was very impressive. Firstly, she located the tip of the organism on my toe which was marked by a tiny dark spot. She set about tearing the toe until the whole structure of the jiga was exposed.

It was surprisingly not painful even without anesthetics local or whole. Eventually, with the tearing of the toe a bit, the organism called jiga was pulled out.

It had a colour like cream and a roundish sinister look. It was one affliction that I suffered along with others during the war. In some, all their toes were perforated by jiga. It was awful. It was a terrible sight to behold. Many others went about with jiga perforated legs and considered it the least of their worries. This shook me very much. Even as I write, I still wonder at the things I saw because of their bizarre nature and what propelled them.

I still ponder how jiga found its way into my toe, lodged there, and grew as far as it was when extracted. I remembered my slipper I lost way back in 1968 as we ran to the forest. I had no other footwear in the war, no wonder this organism found its way to my feet and lodged there.

The things I saw frightened me. At many points, it was like one was in a nightmare and in a hurry to wake up and walk out of it. The events to my young mind were simply crazy and beyond comprehension in the least sense.

The eating of food without salt was always without any meaningful interpretation or explanation. The shooting of a fowl in our homestead by two soldiers and other events in the war made me wonder and ponder how we made it in the war. It therefore made me full of thanksgiving to God that my family survived the war.

In the Christmas of 1969, we went to church at St. Mary's Catholic Church Obibi Ezena on a Sunday. Some nurses at Fr. Kelly's sick bay upon seeing me and my two brothers, wondered aloud about the fact that there were still children like us around.

This was in apparent comparison to a situation when hunger and kwashiorkor had ravaged and devastated our numbers that the children of besieged Biafra were reduced to skeletons and bones.

We smiled and walked past the nurses into the church. They took another look at my two brothers who were ahead of me. It became obvious that the remarks of the nurses were right, I witnessed it. They walked ahead of me strong and dark devoid of the discolorations that came with kwashiorkor and hunger.

We still had some of our dresses that we came back from Onitsha with. We still had shoes which Mum preserved till then. It was only providence that did it for us.

CHAPTER 8

FR KELLY'S SICK BAY

This story will be incomplete without the mention of Fr. Kelly. His contributions and efforts to help in the war were probably the reason why many children and the elderly were spared from the scourge of kwashiorkor and hunger.

His sick bay was a heaven of sorts without the bliss. It offered some semblance of succor and help to many, the hungry, the dying, and those who became destitute by the war found some succor here.

Fr. Kelly was a catholic priest and the parish priest of St. Mary's Catholic Church of Obibi Ezena in the war years. He was from Ireland. In addition to his priestly roles, he delved into taking care of the numerous hungry, malnourished, sick children and adults. He established a sick bay in one of the unused school buildings in the town called Development Primary School.

Over a short time, it became a very popular place among the town's people. It acted as both a hospital and where food was cooked and dispensed to the many hungry people and the destitute. As drugs were dispensed to the sick, food was also dispensed to the hungry.

Nurses and paramedics were engaged therein. I did not have the privilege of seeing a doctor. The sick bay was full of activity at any time. The sick especially those with kwashiorkor were brought here to receive some help. There were many of them. We usually went to the sick bay to get food ourselves.

Fr. Kelly used to share cornmeal with everybody. On such days, information was sent out from the catechist to the town criers that made up Obibi-Ezena. The town criers in turn disseminated the information to the villages. It was that corn meal was going to be shared on such a day. Everybody looked forward to the day with eagerness. The time was usually kept for 3 pm.

Before that time, the field of St. Mary's Catholic Church was already filled with hungry and malnourished people waiting for corn meal with their plates in hand.

It was a bizarre spectacle to behold. The people came with tattered clothes. Many looked like zombies, with heads without hair or hairs that were sickly discolored. The distended stomachs of some with kwashiorkor and the legs of some that were dripping were very evident. Such legs having broken open from edema were mainly all you could see.

The people stood in their different stages of sickness induced by malnutrition. The expectation was very high. If you missed it, you would have to wait for a long time again before another round of corn meal would be shared. Who knows if one would be alive to see another day of grace as this? It was so sad that a majority of the people who stood here would never be around again when Fr. Kelly was going to share corn meal again.

It was a very sorry sight to behold. It looked like it was a parade that could best be compared with characters in a horror movie. The distended stomachs of many, the unnatural discoloration of the pigments and the hair, and the walking skeletons as humans were a compendium of what represented pure horror.

The brightness in most eyes was like it was going to flicker out the next minute. That all came and stood and awaited the meal, was a completion of the horror picture or story. And so, we waited patiently for the meal.

Obibi-Ezena was made up of four villages. The invitation however extended beyond this. St. Mary's Catholic Church as a parish was made up of ten towns. Another name it was referred to was 'Mba-iri' parish. This meant that St. Mary's parish was made up of ten towns.

Fr. Kelly was the parish priest of this 'Mba-iri' parish and the invitation was for everyone therein. So, people from outside Obibi Ezena came too.

As we awaited this meal of life, which to some was like 'viaticum' for they would not be around next time. There was palpable excitement and apprehension in the air. There was noise too as plates and spoons that we came with clanged. We were made to stand in lines according to our villages.

There was a woman then who was called Nda Cathy. People loved her corn meal because of the way she prepared it. So many people preferred to stand before her because she prepared the corn meal better than the other shearers.

So, on these days out of the crowd a song came on:

Ole nde n'eshi anti
Kwashiorkor
Egbelu n'eshi anti
Kwashiorkor
Okporoko eye hu eye,
Cornmeal nwo achahu manu
ke nda Cathy kacha nma,
ericha achokoro.

The song As We Contrived says:
Who are those
That cook anti
Kwashiorkor food,
It is Egbelu
That cooks anti kwashiorkor,

Their stockfish is not soft,
Their corn meal was not
coloured red enough with palm oil
Nda Cathy's own was the best
You would always ask for more.

So the woman called Nda Cathy was preferred because of her cooking ability reflected in the tastiness of her corn meal. Everyone looked forward to eating her corn meal. As we were made to stand in a single file, Nda Cathy's line was the longest.

Fr. Kelly moved around with his pronounced 'k' leg. He ensured that all was well and everyone got a share of the corn meal that might be the only meal for the majority of the people for a long time.

Fr. Kelly's sick bay played these roles. I saw many sick and dying people who were hopelessly admitted here. The outpatient department was very busy. Many that were malnourished and in the firm grips of kwashiorkor came to be treated therein.

But there was not much of a medical solution to their plight towards a desired result. The requisite drugs and their administration were not available for the numerous sick ones. The only drug that was always available was the red-colored roundish tablet called 'Fersolate'. It was reddish. It was commonly used for the treatment of deficiency syndromes like anemia.

We were told it was going to boost one's blood levels and supply the substances that were missing, thereby ensuring good health and escape from the cruel grips of kwashiorkor, malnutrition, and imminent death.

This was the medical sense which made the rounds and which we all believed in. It was readily dispensed to all and sundry. There was a steady supply of this Fersolate for a time.

Kwashiorkor was indeed a very big scourge. It ravaged the population like fire in the harmattan season. There were not enough weapons to fight it; such as knowledge, finances, and international support.

So, it went on and many people sadly died because of it. Food and its availability which would have denied it entrance into our lives, was deliberately made to be unavailable. Hunger and her ally kwashiorkor reigned and ruled over us like a colossus, ensuring we were thoroughly consumed.

My cousins Mathew and Anna were thus consumed. Anna became yellowish like a plant that was covered from sunlight. She was fair already. But her complexion changed. Her legs swelled and at a time burst. And so, it was that I woke up one morning and she could not wake up too. She had become stiff in death having died in the night. Kwashiorkor had claimed her. They carried her and buried her in the backyard without the dignity of a coffin. It was just another emotionless loss of the season.

I stood at her graveside as she was lowered in it wrapped with her mum's disused wrapper. Her mother cried, her eyes bloodshot. I looked away. I could not look at her in her misery. It was like that those days.

Her younger brother quickly followed in the same path of death. We had played and rollicked together with thoughts and visions of what life was going to be like. But the hangman of the destinies of the children of the Southeast let loose by the unfortunate war, cut down many destinies including those of my cousins.

So, Mathew died too like her elder sister with the same obvious symptoms that we had come to hate to see. When it was seen, Fr. Kelly's sick bay was considered but was even like a passage to death or Sheol. It offered no solutions to the problems at hand, especially hunger which was at the root of the whole problem.

And so, at Fr. Kelly's sick bay, it was not much of a tremendous help. People still died in their numbers. I went there once to look around. It was during the corn meal sharing day. We went inside the sick bay to look around out of curiosity. The place looked like any other place than a sick bay. People lay forlornly on the floor with their wrappers or mats as their bed, like there was an epidemic that had stricken many. And they lay in varying degrees of affliction and dying.

The place had an awful smell that was a source of serious health concern and discomfort.

The people clung to hope that was not present nor coming. They looked on for help that was not ever going to smile at them. It was like a drowning man stretching out to grab a rope that turned out to be non-existent or at best imaginary. It was very cruel.

The sick bay became like a morgue of sort, where people were brought and left to die. It was like a refuse bin where people were taken to be disposed of.

Many who were brought here on admission never made it home alive again. The sanitary situation of the sick bay was terrible. There was excrement that littered the back side of the bay. The excrement of those who had loose stomachs brought about by dysentery or cholera was all there was. It littered the immediate back side of the sick bay.

One had to meander or jump to avoid marching those that littered the ground. It sounded unbelievable but so did it also seem that the unfortunate situation that hoisted this on us precipitated and was not showing signs of abating or a let up.

But there, the people lay dying of hunger next to their excrement because their strength was gone and they could not afford to take any other step in their lives that was going to flicker out like a candle on a very windy day.

But there was still a glimmer of hope lighted when Fr. Kelly's sick bay was mentioned despite obvious filthiness and death. People still came expectantly to get help that was sadly not there. It was the desperation that marked our days then. As drowning men and women, we clung to anything even straw for our precious lives. Many did not make it as I saw. It was wicked that we were made to go through this situation.

At a point, the sick bay closed down. It was greeted with sorrow and a sense of utter helplessness. It seemed the only hospital we had, had closed down. There were no others and it did not seem like any other was going to come on the scene. We were left without any hospital or any semblance of it. It was devastating.

It was incomprehensible why this suffering was hoisted on the people. The cornmeal sharing had since stopped. Fr Kelly was not getting any more relief to share. The relief agencies were no longer bringing relief materials from where Fr. Kelly was getting the corn meals he shared with the people. We have been tied to the stakes as Shakespeare said but bearlike, we must fight the course.

These things I saw informed me that the world had no morality. The faces of the starving children meant nothing to the world. It seemed countries got involved in conflicts based on where their interest lay. If it does not concern or enhance 'national interest', it was best left untouched.

The country looked the other way while atrocities were committed and people died. Even if it meant that a whole race had to be wiped out, it was ignored as long as it did not impinge on the overall interest of the country.

America had been held by the public in a distorted manner of her actions abroad. According to (Roy. M. Malcom) in a journal titled; The American Response to the Nigerian Conflict, 1968. Opined that America was viewed as the conscience of the world, exercising a kind of police power where such power might be safely exercised.

If this be the case, she could not find the people of Biafra human enough to perform the roles that had been appropriated to her rightly or wrongly.

America did not come hard on the federal side during the war because it saw Nigeria as a key ally in the fight against communist influences in Africa in the days of the Cold War.

If this be the case, does it justify the death of about 3 million people in reverence to some policy or ideology?

It cannot be overlooked that as America looked at Nigeria as a commercial block that should not be destabilized for her commercial interest, does it also justify the death of over 3 million people as America watched because of some commercial interests and considerations.

The refusal of America to intervene in the case of Biafra citing the internal affairs of Nigeria, would have also made sense that the entire Biafra population was wiped out as America and the world watched. So that it would not be that they intervened in the internal affairs of another country.

Despite the overwhelming evidence of starvation occasioned by a deliberate blockade of the Biafra enclave, America could not intervene more than she did because their national interest was not impinged upon.

The deliberate blockade that killed many people could not be said that the world did not notice it. America which had played the role of being the conscience of the world, refused to intervene more than it did while defenseless civilians were massacred by hunger occasioned by the infamous blockade of the Biafra enclave in the civil war.

CHAPTER 9

THE LIZARDS, FROGS AND SHREW AS ALTERNATIVES

The situation had become desperate and called for desperate measures as well. My eldest brother was a mass server in the days of Fr. Kelly at the parish center. Early in the morning, while I was still asleep, he left for morning mass there.

He was twelve years old. He had a friend who was called Norbert. Both of them were altar boys and served in Fr. Kelly's masses. This was not much of interest to me or my elder brother. We were young and were not qualified for this service. We were rather more concerned with what our eldest brother Mbanugo brought home as he came back from morning mass.

At the back of the parish house was an underground water tank. The water needs of the parish house were satisfied by this water tank to a great extent. A manual pump was attached to the wall of the story building and pumped water to Fr. Kelly's living quarters upstairs. It was in this underground tank that our overall interest lay.

Frogs which we called 'akiri' were many in this tank. After morning mass, Mbanugo and his friend Norbert went to the tank to catch some.

It was hard catching them. If the sun came up sufficiently, the frogs warmed up and were so energized that it became harder to catch them. But it was usually in the morning after morning mass. The sun was not high enough and the heat was not hurting yet. So, he usually caught just a few.

When he came home, we took out the frogs, dissected them, and roasted them. It was a relish to eat the frog, especially the thighs. The thighs were full of muscles. It was contested who should have it. So, we had it in turn.

One had today and another the following day. It was where the meat was. We ate because we were encouraged by our mother who turned a blind eye to it.

She knew better to do so. The lack of protein in our food was the reason among others why we were malnourished and the resultant kwashiorkor.

So, she tacitly encouraged us. Lizards came to the rescue as one of the sources whereby we augmented our protein sources. We hunted them deliberately. We set traps to catch them and made them part of our distasteful menu.

The only part we could not eat was the head. We cut it off took out the entrails and we were good to go.

It was not funny in any sense of it having to eat lizard. It was bitter if not properly seasoned. But mum encouraged us to drink this bitter elixir that held the solution to our survival; escape from the distended tummy, kwashiorkor, and eventual death. We made broth out of the lizards we caught.

We bid our spirits avouch the fact that we were eating lizards, we had paid no attention to before now. The broth was close to being bitter more so when it was saltless and was really like a bitter drug that one must drink to live on.

The yellowish pebble-sized eggs of lizards attracted our attention too. We painstakingly identified female lizards and the place where they laid eggs. We identified and dug out the eggs. We roasted them in the fire.

The crunchy sound of the roasted lizards' eggs melted away in our hungry mouths. We did not worry any bit about whether the eggs were edible or not for as we ate the mothers that laid the eggs and survived, we thought nothing really of the small pebble-sized yellowish eggs of the lizards doing us any harm.

You might find this unbelievable or at best melodramatic. But the days were like no other and therefore desperate measures were employed to satisfy the demands of those days that belonged to infamy. It was the reason and that of providence that I stand today to give an account of those desperate days. I was not left to be carried away by kwashiorkor on a very dirty platter.

Even the likes of smelly shrews that age-long restriction and their terrible odour had prevented us from eating, took pride of place in our menu. But the craziness of the situation we found ourselves in, had made us romance with what was a taboo and relished in it as it graced our enameled plates during meals with her pointed snout like a swordfish.

So, shrew (nkapi) came to be included in our meals. We hunted and killed it. Its smell was awful. But we commanded our spirit to avouch it. The exigencies of the situation demanded it. We simply obeyed having no choice but to.

It was like there was a gang up against us by both man and nature. The lizards that used to be uncountable on walls hitherto were suddenly gone. Could it be we had finished the stock of lizards or was it that the walls had no more lizards to display?

The hunt for them however intensified, assumed a more serious dimension, requiring skill that people my age did not possess any longer. Some boys came from neighboring towns and villages who were special lizard hunters.

They got close to the wall and wriggled a brightly coloured object up where the lizards could see it. The lizards ran out to catch it. The brightly coloured bait was mistaken to be an insect. The lizards ran to get it. The boys stretched out their hands in a fast manner and caught the lizard. It quickly disappeared into a bag that was already becoming full with the reptile.

We did not possess this skill of catching them. So, we watched from the sidelines as our stock of food was soon depleted and there were no restocking contingencies.

Grasshopper which we called (koloko) was another food we had. Their coming was seasonal and somehow coincided with the crisis's periods. At their appearance, it was a source of joy. We caught and roasted them. If we caught many, we fried them and put them in our soup that was bereft of salt.

In the soup, therefore, roasted or fried grasshopper filled it. It gave us a semblance of some well-being. The desperate nature of those days cannot be overemphasized.

Therefore, as a kid, I went with others to the forest to catch grasshoppers which we also called 'Oshinaka'. We rummaged deep inside the forest in search of them.

Our soup's taste and appetite depended on them when the others like lizards or shrews were not available. They replaced meat and fish which were not available. We have gone without protein for a long time. So, the appearance of 'Oshinaka' was a very welcome respite.

All of us went with one container or the other to the forest to catch as much as we could. Smiles momentarily played around our lips. It boosted or revived the local food industry. People who caught many fried and had baskets of it. This was taken to the Orie Obibi market and sold or bartered for what they didn't have.

God was really on our side despite all that happened. Such things as 'Oshinaka' and other bizarre things we ventured into but lived to tell of our experiences could have been only God's intervention that kept harm away.

So as the times ticked away and our heart beat ticked along too, our concern was all about our overall safety. The guns boomed away, kwashiorkor reigned and hunger took hold of our days and reigned without any challenge.

CHAPTER 10

THE UNCONVENTIONAL DELIVERY

It was unimaginable what happened before me one day. It looked like fables or at worst from a melodramatic narrative. If I had not been involved, it would seem as such that events and situations that characterized those days would still lie hidden.

My narrative even from the eyes of infancy beheld much bizarre and unconventional events. How then would it be if an adult in my level or class during the war decided to put his observations and experiences on paper? A lot surely would be known as per the senseless war that engulfed us as fire, diminished, and emasculated us as a people.

As has been said, those days were characterized by strange things that were very far from the norm. I woke up one morning to a commotion that was in front of my father's house.

I got out and hurried to see what it was that was making news and bringing about a commotion. I did not want to be told what had happened by a third party. I also learned that survival in these times depended upon how fast one reacted to situations as they unfolded. Our escape before this had depended on prompt reaction. It was lessons we had learned before now. Many have died because of careless attitude to situations that turned out to be grave which required prompt reaction.

So it was that the majority of the people that gathered were women. They formed a cordon around a woman they did not want others to see.

This aroused my curiosity more and I got closer. I peeped inside the circle that was formed by the women. There was increased activity both inside and outside the cordon. Someone quickly brought a wrapper to make the cordon impenetrable so that no one could see what was going on inside of it.

Shortly after, the shrill cry of a baby broke the cold morning peace, broke into our thoughts, interrupted the stream of our consciousness. It was a woman that was giving birth in such a bizarre manner in our kindred.

He chose this early morning to come. Even as war and its agent, hunger, were dutifully depleting our numbers, reducing our strength as a people, new births were still being recorded like the one I just witnessed. This child was the third child of a man in our homestead we called Nda Ihie-Ukwu.

At the sound of the shrill cry of the baby, there was a break out of joyous singing and dancing by the women. This was like an interlude in a period of long brutal keenness.

It was a good distraction from the long attention which the war had made us have. Occasions like this were welcome despite the exigencies of the times. So, this Child's birth brought a much-needed interlude in a very serious situation. It played the role of a comic relief.

And so, it was that the women rose with wild jubilation and ululation.

> Eh eh eh eh eh eh eh!
> Oro nwa o.
> Omuru nwa nini,
>
> Omuru nwa nwoke o
>
> (What is the sex of the baby?
> She gave birth to a baby boy.)

This rent and shattered the morning's peace. The air raids and the war were temporarily forgotten. The women danced and gyrated their stiffened hips that had long lost a reasonable percentage of their flesh as a result of hunger.

'Obere ma nwa
Onye ga enyem',
(If not for a child who would give a mother).

The women sang to the admiration of those who watched. The sorrows and the events of the past were temporarily forgotten as was said. But like the gazelle at the water hole, we reserved one ear that searched for when it would start again when the fighter planes would roar out of the sky again with their deadly cargoes to pelt us with.

Biam biam ka mma n' ole
Biam biam ka mma n'ehie (twice)

Ya bina gi ya biana m
Biam biam ka mma n'ehie (twice)
(Where is the best place for massaging,
It is best in the groin,
When you are massaged,
It becomes my turn to be massaged)

The women were ecstatic with joy. It surprised me beyond description. Some of them had just buried their children that kwashiorkor claimed and had no reason to be happy at all. But here they stood and danced without a care in the whole world with one determination; to do justice to the age-long attachment to new babies and the process of welcoming them into a world that was riddled with great evil and death.

The war was not able to put a stop to this. As moods can infect, all of us became happy and hilarious at the exhibition of joy at the birth of another child into the world.

The men especially Nda Ihie Ukwu the husband of the woman, at the news of his wife's safe delivery, came to the men clustered a distance away, raised his hands in the air like he was saluting the air:

"Meeki manu"

The men bellowed in Unisom with excitement in their eyes and smile playing around their shrunken faces, shouted.

"Hoos"

This he repeated a couple of times, each time assuming a more artistic and creative disposition and posture.

Such events as described marked our days. Our moments of sorrow were interspersed with brief interludes of joy and happiness. Despite the current state of happiness, we did not forget we were still embroiled in a fratricidal war and soon the agents of death would come looking for us to silence our joy and make us sad again.

I was however so surprised that right before my presence, a child was born in no other place than in the middle of our homestead as the mid-morning sun watched and raffia trees waved in approval. People were happy at the event that had given a very small respite for joy despite the onslaught of the federal army.

The solidarity of the women shown towards their own was splendid. I was so surprised at the way they quickly gathered and covered this scene. It was Novell to me.

It was not long afterward that we fell back to the frightening routine and apprehension that marked the times. The child's mother and her husband had to worry about how to feed the child. It was left for them to worry about how to ensure that the breast was full for the baby to be suckled other than a flabby and empty breast riddled with veins. It was a real cause for concern. It was a common lesson that out of necessity, exist lots of possibilities.

I never ceased to wonder why the birth took place outside in the open while there were huts to be used. Was it because of the madness of the times that ensured it was so? It defied my understanding and made me review the events of those days critically.

Another of these events was when we became very friendly with one of the federal soldiers. While we were living with the federal soldiers when Owerri was captured. The people of our village interacted warmly with one federal soldier who became very friendly with almost the entire members of the village.

He told us his name was Samari. He mixed freely with everyone and was never given to discriminating against us. It was while he interacted with us that we learnt about his philosophy of life. He was a man who believed in non-violence and was therefore its disciple.

He told us that his mother told him not to kill anyone before he set off for the war and that so far, he had carried out this injunction to the latter.

In the war front he did not shoot anyone but pointed his gun upwards and shot into the air. These were some of the things he told us. Perhaps, if it was only him, there would not have been a war.

There was however no way we could verify his claims. But it made us have lots of respect and admiration for this man who came to fight our people without the intention of killing anyone.

This was in comparison to the carnage and massacre of our kith and kin that had taken place before our presence in the hands of his brethren. It could not be ascertained if this was a decoy but to a great extent, we believed Samari.

But one day Samari was shot and killed by a Biafran sniper in a tall and bushy tree almost in the center of the market place. His over sized boots gave him away as he noisily walked towards his group to catch up with them back as they went back to their location in Owerri in the twilight of the day. That was how Samari died in a terrible twist of irony.

He was buried by the road before the market. His grave was very shallow indeed for after a short time he died and was resultantly interred, his grave started gushing out oil.

As I passed on the road to the market, the grave of Samari gushed oil that covered a reasonable portion of the road. It's not like a case of speaking ill of the dead but the case of this man was pathetic to me.

As a child, I met him and got to know him. It was only sheer skepticism that stopped me from shaking his hands. While other children and the elderly related with him, I was kept back from joining in the fray that Samari occasioned and was at the center of. But there he lay on the road in a very shallow grave that could not contain him but threatened to push out as the fat of his body spilled and stained the road.

It amazed me at the trend of events in the war that someone who pursued an agenda of nonviolence was cut down by the very thing he was told not to practice and that had come to settle in his soul as a way to go. It did not enlighten my understanding any bit but made me more confused and looking for answers.

In the conflict, I was confronted with things, issues that I ordinarily would not have met nor encountered in my entire life. Situations of a very bizarre nature confronted me and not only me but each of us in the besieged Biafra.

Samari was one of them. Such memories as his were etched in my mind forever. Posterity would only judge such matters as Samari laid before us. I would not attempt even to judge or lay any blame on any of those matters that confronted us as a people. But frankly, the likes of Samari did not make much meaning to me even as a toddler.

My dear mother was another phenomenon that eluded my total comprehension. At best, I considered her an enigma. She possessed all it took to sustain any accolade she could be addressed with.

We were spared the disease of the time probably by her foresight and good judgment of hers, armed with requisite knowledge and assistance that could have only come from God.

An example was kwashiorkor. It was the mark of the day for all families and children. There were not probably many families that were spared the devastation that kwashiorkor brought. I told of how cousins of mine were killed by kwashiorkor. One was taken to Uzo-agba where a rehabilitation center was established to take care of very hopeless cases of the scourge.

My two brothers and I were spared the ordeal of this sickness. We were going at full steam like a ship would on a very rough sea. Mother was always up in the morning like the woman of Proverbs 31 and ensured all was well with us. She went to very distant markets of very far lands to barter some materials we still had. She traveled to places like Odufo in present-day Rivers state.

On the days of the market days, she and her fellows would have been tracking the day like one would a satellite. They rose early about 4 a.m. In conjunction with others, they departed for this market that was far away. Her coming back was usually late in the night. They would have trekked to and fro, a distance of about 35 kilometers.

However, distant markets far into the interiors of present-day River state such as Odufo, etc., held some very slim hope that salt could be seen or some other precious commodities like fish which we desperately needed.

She went with some items like glass cups, brakeable plates, and clothes which she battered with whoever needed them. The Biafran currency was not much help in these matters. She did not spare any effort in ensuring we were kept safe from the destructions occasioned by kwashiorkor.

When we lived in Onitsha, as our lives were starting, we had lots of clothes that we came to the village with when war broke out. It was these dresses that my mother kept selling in these distant markets to batter for other goods we did not have, salt especially.

A day came when I particularly asked for one of my dresses. It was the same type of dress for us all. So, when I asked Mum for my dress to wear, she smiled and told us,

"When you were licking salt and eating food where did you think the money came from".

Mum sold some of our dresses for us to feed and especially to buy salt wherever it was sighted. She said it with smiles playing around her face. We laughed along with her.

The truth was that our clothes were being sold to get the things we did not have in the house. Her death in 2009 was a loss that could not be quantified in any way.

The recovery of her white bicycle bore a great eloquence to her tenacity. Mum's bicycle was commandeered by a man who was a captain in the Biafran army. He took the bicycle to somewhere in Rivers State where he was posted. Mum did a lot to recover the bicycle from this man irrespective of the risks involved in those days. She went to the man despite his being a Biafran army captain who could make life difficult for her to a great extent.

My mother was therefore willed and equally bold. She stood for what she believed in and was ready to die for it. She was enlightened to a great extent.

One of her greatest worries during the war was how to secure her jewelry and her wrappers. She had quite a reasonable number of them. She could not sit and let the wrappers be stolen or fall into the hands of the wrong people.

In front of our house were blocks my father made to build a house. One night some people she hired came and took the blocks apart for they were many. They took her box of wrappers, for it was also in a metal box, and put it in the block and brought the blocks back in place.

The wrappers were there until the war ended. Mum's wisdom never failed her. But something was wrong with this one. When they brought out the wrappers, they were brittle from heat and moisture. It was no small loss for her. It was counted as one of the things she lost during the war.

At the end of the war, she went on to become a business tycoon with an interest in transportation and construction. She died in 2009 at age 75.

The days skidded further into more hopelessness. The osere phenomenon as described earlier was now a recurring sight. They were being pushed out almost daily and it was a measure of which ground we held and lost.

Judging from the recurrence of these, we were losing a lot of ground. There was a lot of pressure on us from all sides. Food was at this juncture scarce.

There was no rest for anyone as none could guarantee his safety or be in control of what happened the next minute. The times went crazy.

Kids were forcibly taken to assist in the war effort. My eldest brother was always apprehended to help in carrying food to our soldiers at the war front.

It was always moments of great fear and apprehension for Mum, fearing for her twelve-year-old son. It showed how critical things were for our Biafran state. Even at 12 years old, he was no longer given to walking about freely but was always on the lookout for those who would come to conscript him. He was young and tender for that kind of role.

The federal soldiers that occupied our land hurriedly left like they were chased out. We were living in a Biafra-occupied territory once more.

Our soldiers once more interacted with us and did a lot of reassurances. We were therefore better apprised of situations at the war front with the Biafran soldiers living with us.

Things were so hard so much that bicycles ran on bare wheels without tires. People still rode on them with bags of garri on their way to liberated Owerri which was once more under Biafra's control.

Salt had been scarce before but now it was not available anywhere.

Meals time was a very uninteresting moment for all especially me. Mum augmented with 'Ogiri'in the absence of salt.

'Ogiri' was a traditional condiment that was made with things that made it have a dispelling or putrid odour. It was used in the soup. It took the place of salt and fish and seasoner. As much as I was concerned, it was not a good replacement at all.

Meat was not even remembered anymore. The sight of meat was like an apparition that was not sought for. With the recapture of Owerri, it was generally believed that things were going to be better and that victories would continue from one city to another until the federal troops were chased out of Biafra's territory.

We were happy with the news of the victories of the Biafra air force. It was welcome news and in addition to that, we were relieved that some mercenaries had joined and became part of the force. We were simply elated.

Our drooping spirits were revived with this piece of news. We expectantly awaited the news that never came of the continued victory of our forces over our invaders. The good news was always short-lived, for we were afterward inundated with gory details from the war front.

According to (Osuji, Steve 2012), such feats of Biafra forces as the Abagana ambush of March 25, 1968, was about the most memorable day in Nigeria- the Biafra war. "It was the day the Nigerian side suffered the heaviest single loss in the war known as the Abagana ambush. The second division of the Nigerian army led by Col. Murtala Mohammed had finally crossed the Niger Bridge after failing in the first attempts (having been repelled by the Col. Joe Achuzia guerrilla army and suffering heavy causalities)." According to (Achebe's There Was a Country) the Biafra's strategy under Major Uchendu proved to be highly successful. "His troops destroyed Muhammed entire convoy within one and a half hours. All told, the Nigerians suffered about 500 casualties. There was minimal loss on the Biafran side."

The news however continued to come about our abilities that

stunned the enemy. This excited us and gave us hope that victory was going to be ours.

The information also reached us of our locally made weapons that were a pride of the Biafran army and her people. The ogbunigwe was one weapon developed by Biafra that was dreaded by the enemy. It was so dreaded by the enemy that professor Chukwuemeka Ike in his book Sunset at Dawn; a novel about Biafra, captures it," you must have heard that the Nigerians are now so mortally afraid of ogbunigwe that each advancing battalion is now preceded by a herd of cattle".

I took particular exception to information that our ingenuity in improvisation and acts of gallantry at the war front were hampered in one way or the other. This brought painful setbacks in the progress of the war.

There was a lot of unverifiable information which reached us daily. We had no way of authenticating them but they oiled our ego all the same and assured us that all was going to be alright after all.

But lately, the plethora of bad news increased more than we heard the positive ones. It made us very sad and made us think about our overall survival as individuals and as a people.

It was in one of these situations that we heard that planes had sadly stopped landing at our treasured Uli airstrip. It was a grave concern to us all. In retrospect, it became clear why things became so scarce and hunger reigned. It was part of a death knell that led to an eventual capitulation in my thoughts.

All the doggedness and brilliance that Biafra exhibited had failed to turn the tide in our favour. The hopes and expectations dissipated like dew in the warm morning sun.

All the ambushes that briefly halted the federal army's advances into the Biafran enclave were not enough to stop them permanently and guarantee victory for us. It could not save our bid for self-determination. It looked like it was over for our struggle.

I feared gravely when I looked at my mother's face. She was as sad as ever. It affected me and my brothers too, made us stand with uneasiness. Our overall hopes were gradually fading or pouring away as water poured on dunes. It was a miserable time and an apprehensive period in our lives.

It was not expected to come to this in our wildest imaginations. As lay people we all were, we never expected it was going to be this abysmal. Our victory had already been agreed by us, signed by providence, we believed. But here we stood on the threshold of uncertainty and threat of complete annihilation.

The stories of smart weapons that Biafra produced especially 'the Ogbunigwe' that struck awe in the heart of the enemy were relegated to the background and could not help achieve our overall objective. The weapons despite their smartness were not able to tilt the conflict in our overall favour. The 'shore battery' that was deployed to destroy ships elated us and kept our hopes alive. The news of these victories and inventions reached us from the war front and lifted our Morale.

As the news passed from one hand unto another, it became either over-diluted or made to be too hot to be handled and this gave us false hopes. The news however reached us and oiled our morale that victory was surely ours.

Even when the story had been told before, it was usually retold and it brought reassurances that it was well with our cause and it was achievable anyhow. So, the story you have heard before made more sense to you when retold. There was a need for continued reaffirmation of our invincibility in the war as a people.

Even as a child, I had a sense of foreboding, an innate fear I could not pin down. As a kid, I saw the gloom written boldly on my mother's face as has been previously said. She was the mirror upon which I saw what was happening.

During the day, I did not hear any story, I got the same from Mum's countenance. It was scary and discouraging. The fact remained that all was not well with the cause Biafra was pursuing. The prognosis was indeed bad.

So, at the sound of an explosion in the distance, Mum hushed us, 'Guzonu', she said. At this, we kept quiet and Mum searched to know the direction of the explosion and matched it with the possible position our troops maintained or held.

It was usually moments of great apprehension. Our lives were not safe at all in any sense of it. There was no guarantee that we were going to be alive when tomorrow came. A mortar could fall on anyone at any time.

So, it was one day we were playing in the sand at Ama-Orie. We ran to the place to spend a few days. It was not unconnected with running for our safety. Mum had taken us here because our village was too close to the war front that was in Owerri.

So, it was when we heard something whiz past above us. It was seconds later that we heard an explosion in the direction and trajectory of the object that just flew past. It was later discovered that the mortar had fallen in the home of our kith and kin at the next village called Ogbe-ke. It was not without causalities.

So, our lives consisted of uncertainty not knowing what to eat or what would take place the next minute. Whatever happened the next minute was highly unpredictable. We held on for almost three solid years.

There was no letup in what we suffered. Our hopes had risen on the belief and information that all was well with the struggle. But this fell too because it was no longer as expected or foretold.

We had watched our loved ones die in our hands, snatched away from us by the pale hands of death and kwashiorkor. We had also beheld our kith and kin die from weapons of warfare. We had however continued to run, for it was said that 'Osondu agwuike' (the race to escape death is not tiresome). We had continued to run to no place in particular but farther away from the sound of the guns of the approaching federal soldiers.

We had lost all our belongings that meant anything to us. The things that we garnered all our lives, we had lost. Some that remained were in ruins, inconsequential, and of not much use or value anymore.

The ones we still ran along with were greatly of not much value but we clung to them all the same like our lives depended on them.

It has been a time of great self-pity as we ran to nowhere exactly with our rag-tag remains of selves and property. The reason for this whole suffering was no longer a reason to ponder over. All that mattered was just to continue to run until we too drop dead as countless others.

CHAPTER 11

THE LAST FLIGHT

Things had become so hard, confused, and desperate. The atmosphere was heavy, laden with an impending doom for us and of course the young nation called Biafra whose rising sun was still on the horizon and about to set in infancy. People went about with long and fearful faces, there being no need to laugh.

Movements were brisk and hurried amidst hunger. Plans were made of where one had to run to and what generally one had to do. It was a hard decision choosing where to run. The entire Biafran land mass was almost occupied by the federal army. It left only a small fraction of what was the entire country.

The last 'osere' passage through the village informed us that all was not well with our troops. It also informed us of the very grave situation of our existence as a people and of our sovereign status which we had fought to assert for the last three years.

All the Biafra's cities were under the control of federal troops. All the accesses to the enclave were either occupied or cut off. In low tones, the elderly discussed with graveness on their faces. They bemoaned the fate of the setting of Biafra's sun, being forced out of the sky.

They considered the information that was making the rounds that all males were to be killed leaving only the women and girls when the enclave was finally overrun. It was indeed a great source of worry.

What looked like it was not feasible because of our perceived invincibility was becoming a reality with each passage of time even as the guns sounded closer and closer.

They tried to apportion blame as to why the war was going to be lost. The 'Sabo' the shortened word for saboteur was roundly blamed and condemned as being the main reason why the war was on the verge of being lost. We watched as defeat and outright annihilation starred us in the face as victory was eluding us.

The prospect of losing all that was fought for was getting brighter by the minute. The consequences of losing were looming larger on the horizon, like a genie that had escaped from the bottle. So, it was to us.

The elders came together in groups and considered the fate that awaited us as individuals and a people. News of gallantry was no longer coming. When they did, were snuffed out or overshadowed with overwhelming evidence of failures and imminent defeat.

It was obvious the rising sun of Biafra was preparing to set prematurely without at least reaching midday. The young crescent sun had only shone for about three turbulent years and was preparing to go down ignominiously.

It was being forced down by forces greater than her. Not even the audacious recognition of Biafra by some African nations could guarantee the continued existence of the state of Biafra. She was hemmed in from all sides.

The hunger which was recognized as an instrument of war, was unleashed on us, and heavy weaponry was let loose on the people who had started fighting with shotguns. What started as a police action was now a full military matter being decided by well-trained military men from world-class military academies scattered all over the globe.

The effects of all these were evident. The suffering of the people was unprecedented including the writer. We were not spared the agonizing pangs of hunger and the deathly situation which has become like a boring refrain.

We were pounded and hounded from all the theaters of war.

The people waited for whatever fate had in stock for them. It was in exasperation, for there was no place else to go and nothing else to do about this situation that bedeviled us. Some therefore waited for their fate to hand them over to either death or life.

Our hope and emotions were finally dealt a deadly blow when the news reached us that the last plane had ingloriously flown out of Uli with Ojukwu in its belly. It was also said that Col. Effiong was now in the saddle of whatever remained of our dear and embattled Biafra. With Ojukwu out of the way, our morale sank to the bottom. There was no more hope. There was an unprecedented level of despair among the populace.

Preparations were made for the worst in a hurry. Mum consulted others in a series of consultations that usually took place before we ran. That evening was not an exception. She decided after consultations that we should move from our village to Ogwa.

Ogwa is situated off the highway between Owerri and Okigwe. We prepared to run to the place, for it was not advisable to stay when the enemy that hated you so much was advancing.

My mum and others reasoned among themselves. Some people like my uncle Columbus stayed back. He reasoned and tried to impress it upon my mother, that it was no use running anymore. He opined that those who had cars and the means had all gone away.

He insisted that he was not going to be drawn into the futility of doing such things as escaping from the federal army that had really occupied and surrounded everywhere. He advised against it.

But Mum did not buy into these reasons. Her mind was made up and the consultations of previous hours had made her resolved about running out of the village.

I wish she listened to my uncle for our moving out of the village was like a painful merry-go-round. My uncle was usually different about issues. He was alone because of his views that were close to being radical and blunt as well. His opinions in this matter were contrary to the other opinions that pervaded. He stayed back, sticking to his minority view.

And so it was that before night fell, on an overcast evening, we packed a few of our things and left the village in the twilight of the day towards an uncertain future. It was inadvertently the twilight of the nation called Biafra because we came back to our house in a unified Nigeria.

I was carrying an iron bucket, a red transistor radio we owned and other small things that a 9-year-old could carry. The radio was later collected by a federal soldier at a checkpoint while we walked back.

My elder brother Chika carried a box of what remained of our clothes. My eldest brother, Mba-nugo carried Mum's sewing machine and one or two other things.

We had no car nor any form of mobility to move with or facilitate our escape. Our car was disposed of by the beginning of the war. Even if we had it, it would have been impossible to operate or run it in the besieged Biafra. This was because there was no petrol anywhere. But even if it was around, it would have been taken or commandeered by either the Biafran or the Nigerian soldiers.

So, with our loads on our heads and with Mum leading the way, we melted into the twilight of the day. We set off in the direction of Owerri amidst a drizzle.

My uncle watched as we departed the homestead from the small windows of his hut that was close to my father's house. He bluntly refused to run or to reconsider his stance because of his strong belief that it was futile. He stayed back. We met him when we got back the day after.

One other uncle warned that as we were running away, everything we left behind was to be considered abandoned. He reasoned that whatever was left behind was arguably abandoned and should be treated as such. In his estimation, he thought we would not come back alive so he would have a go at the things we left behind.

However, our mother was not deterred by his threats as we took one last look at our hut that stood sorrowfully in the last light of the day and left for safety.

When we left our house, the journey progressed by foot. As we got out of the village, the road soon thinned out into a pathway with thick foliage that lined both sides of the path.

It was getting dark and fast too with a slight drizzle on. Rain-carrying clouds covered the sky and ensured it was so dark without a star in sight. We trudged doggedly and determinedly towards O-gwa about 32 kilometers away.

Others walked along with us but I did not remember who they were. This made our walk through the path not too scary. The pathway had become dark and our slightly darkened images walked along with fireflies beginning to appear. It was a miserable spectacle to behold.

At the outskirts of Na-ze in present-day Owerri west L G A of Imo State, we met our first shocking spectacle of the evening. A family of five lay dead on the road. Their corpses covered with plantain leaves lay forlornly on the road we were passing.

A mortar fell before them and none survived as we gleaned from the scene. People skirted around them and went on their way as the guns boomed not far away. We too skirted by and moved on.

The time was far spent as we approached Owerri, a distance of 7 kilometers.

Darkness had fully descended and everywhere was enveloped in it. The path too was not left out. Thick darkness covered it. We could barely see where we were going. We exercised caution not to bump into one another. It was a very narrow path we were on and were forced to walk in a single file.

The night was a greatly disturbed one. However, we walked quietly towards our destination as fireflies twinkled, making the whole scene eerie especially for us children. The noise of insects filled the air and momentarily took our attention away from the sound of guns that boomed in the distance. We move on tiredly and hungrily like being driven by ruthless taskmasters with their bone-tipped whips.

It has been an overcast evening all along. The clouds were heavy with rain and at a point, rain started falling in ceaseless rhythms and torrents. We could not afford to wait for the rain to cease, and besides, there was no place to wait out the rain. It was in the middle of the forest. We were walking with some apprehension to come out of the forest area before it got very dark. It could be harmful. So, we plodded on in the dark narrow path as the rain poured its water on us.

The spectacle of the family that lay dead behind us was still very fresh to each one of us even as we strived to possibly get out of harm's way. Our teeth clattered and we shivered under the cold rain.

Our apprehension became heightened by the fact that rainwater might have washed out snakes or disturbed their habitat and chased them out from the bush for us to step on. We continued all the same.

Our case was better than the family that lay dead behind us. We walked for about two hours. The rain stopped slightly and was reduced to a slight drizzle again.

We emerged unto a road out of the path from our village. This road was the last approach to Owerri town from our village 7 kilometers behind.

The road was very sandy. This slowed us down considerably. Because of the sandy nature of the road, it was like walking in the desert. Our pace slowed down.

We approached a popular junction called Eke Mba ato. This was on the outskirts of Owerri. It was so called because it connected three towns. It served as a junction but was closest to Owerri town. From the hills on this junction, one could see Owerri as it simmered in the distance especially when you looked in the night. This junction is currently on the busy Aba Owerri Road expressway.

The undulating nature of the road caused me to trip as explosions lighted the night sky. The sandy nature of the road did not also help matters. It required extra strength to move on it. I was simply overcome and tripped and fell.

It had become dark. We groped on in the road as occasional illumination brought about by explosions in the distance lighted the night sky and the way momentarily. Darkness enveloped us again. Uncertainty lay ahead of our future.

The contents of my load spilled on the ground in the darkness. I was pulled up by my mother. The contents of what I carried were gathered up. We had to grope about to re-gather them. She helped me carry the load again as my two brothers watched.

It was almost 10,30pm in the night. The rain had graciously ceased though we were wet to our skin. We were cold.

The sky had become clearer. The moon, crescent-shaped was visible in the sky, rain-carrying clouds still covered her intermittently. Even stars too could be seen twinkling on what became the final day of the 3-year war.

A light breeze blew and rustled the foliage and created the impression that it was being done by people lurking around seeking to harm us. We were apprehensive and suspicious of any movements. It became part of us and existed as a habit in the war.

Having gathered my things that fell on the ground, we soon got to a place called 'Ama-wire' which was on the portion of Okigwe road that is closest to Orji, a suburban of Owerri. It was called 'Ama wire' because of the electricity distribution power line that passed across the road. It is still there today.

It was here that we decided to rest for the night. We could go no further. Both young and old craved for rest. We had gone ahead for four straight hours with our load on our heads, we had become exhausted.

It was by this electric pylon that we chose to rest, overcome by fatigue and hunger. I do not know what informed the decision to stop at this juncture of all places. However, it was sheer pain to stand any more on our feet. We had walked for about four hours and were really tired and reasonably worn out.

So, under the high-tension electric cables, by the side of the road, we decided to stop and rest for the night. It was 11.30 pm in the night. I do not know why we chose this place to make our bed despite the obvious dangers of being under an electric pylon and in a condition of extreme wetness on a rainy evening.

In hindsight, I was sure that there was no power in the electric line which was brought about by the war. So, the power lines were mere structures that had no life. Little wonder why we decided to stay under it for the night.

We did not come along with mats or any such to place on the floor for sleeping. What served as mats were mum's wrappers we spread on the wet floor. There was no other choice or way out of this than Mum's wrapper, we spread on the wet floor. This beckoned on us to lie on as we were reasonably very tired.

The wrappers on the floor despite their wetness and unwholesomeness looked very inviting. I could not wait to lie on it and relieve my body from the pains that were wracking it.

We lay down on the wrappers. I was closest to Mum and my elder brother came after and the eldest. We shared the warmth that emanated from our cold bodies and stayed so in fitful sleep until morning came and met us still huddled together in ascending order.

We had our last meal far before we left the hut in the village. We had no other thing to eat. We were hungry but there being nothing to do about it, we slept. It was also why our sleep was fitful.

It was a very hard day. We were not ever subjected to this kind of situation since. This particular night was the climax of all that we had continued to go through. It was like a culmination of all we had seen in the entire war. Our stay in the forest and other harrowing experiences we had, could not be compared with what we were going through this very night. But a certain hope still urged us on. Undaunted by weakness and hunger, we plodded on according to the leading of this certain hope and promise of life ahead.

The rain as said had ceased and allowed us to spread our wrappers on the wet ground in the open and slept. Morning came rather very quickly with the sun already coming up from the horizon and bathing the whole place with her very comforting heat. We woke up. It was a deserved rest given the ordeal of the previous evening. We were about 25 kilometers to our destination and had to leave again and early too.

After the meals, we were strengthened and ready to continue the journey.

Our journey to our destination Ogwa continued on a very tired and apprehensive note. Ogwa was about 25 kilometers from where we were and we trudged on towards an uncertain future in the direction of the town.

There was no presence of the federal army which was the real attraction of the place. Many others flocked to this place because of the above reason. It was way down in the evening when the sun had gone down that we arrived there.

All along as we walked on, the guns boomed and made our getting away more urgent. We walked all day and rested very briefly. This was out of eagerness to get away from the guns that boomed and were getting nearer and nearer.

The road was filled with desperate people who were equally trying to get away from the war. There was a sense of urgency in the movement of every one as it was with us.

The road was devoid of vehicular traffic apart from one or two vehicles that ran grandiosely by amidst a horde of disgruntled refugees and their tattered selves walking away from danger. So, the road was.

It was a long tortuous journey. Thirsty and hungry, we plodded on eager to get away from the situation. The guns got closer and closer approached like a category 3 storm.

Everyone ran, for no one wanted to be caught in the crossfire. Our safety was ultimate. As long as our legs could still carry us, we went on towards where we thought was going to be safe from the onslaught of the federal army.

Mum urged us on. She encouraged us and told us that all surely was going to be well. It was a false hope that came from parents not backed up by any visible positivity. It all looked very gloomy all around.

I did not know where she was borrowing her strength from. Even though what she was telling us was a lie, we still believed it and were strengthened by it nonetheless.

At the junction of Ogwa town, we branched off and headed left towards the town. It was late in the evening when we arrived. We had trekked all day with the food we ate in the morning, and stopped at brief moments to rest. We were so tired when we got there.

And so, it was that we finally got there. We faced another problem that starred us in the face. Because of the numerous refugees who ran into the town, we could not find a place to sleep. We had no relatives here. It was purely out of no other option that we came here in the first place.

Hotels were out of it being a small town and the war did not support such opulence as hotels. The thought of a hotel in these times and places was indeed preposterous and out of place.

There was commotion in the town generally as the impending attack of the federal forces filled the air and filled us with trepidation and uncertainty. The town was rowdy with many other refugees who had come to seek refuge in the town like us. It was therefore almost heavily overcrowded.

It had become dark being around 8 p.m. Mum was gravely concerned about where we would sleep and rest after a long walk from Owerri to Ogwa. She looked for a place while we waited with our loads upon our heads.

No one obliged to give us where to sleep as Mum passionately begged for a space enough for us to sleep and rest for the night. All her entreaties fell on deaf ears. No one listened for no space was really available to be given out.

The last man she approached was so kind but had no place to offer us other than his goat's pen. It was the only space he had left. There were however no goats in the pen. This was to our overall advantage. It was why the man gave us in the first instance.

And so, to the goat's pen, we went almost with a trot lest the man changed his mind. I liked the accommodation because I was well below the low roof of the pen. It was only my mother and my eldest brother who did not find the low roof of the pen accommodating. Mum was not complaining despite obvious reasons. She profusely thanked our host for the accommodation and we started settling down to our new abode, sweeping and cleaning.

Our new house smelt of the goats that inhabited it and generally of the habitation of animals. We were contented to dwell here than worried about the odour or anything else. There was no other alternative that came our way. It did not matter to us if it was the habitation of animals. We were happy to stay here. We had gone through harder times; this was nothing compared to the side of the road we slept last night on a wet floor. Our forays into the forest in search of safety had made us know what extremities of situations were. The goat's pen was not impossible.

So, we settled in for the night after we swept and cleaned, making it a bit useable. Soon I was overcome by fatigue and exhaustion; I fell asleep fast and woke in the morning. Everyone else crashed as I did. Morning still found us alive, hale and hearty.

Events were taking place faster than we were able to keep up with. Even as we were settling down in the goat's pen, the bloody three-year war of Biafra was about to end.

Our stay in the goat's pen as refugees was only for one night. The night was uneventful but surely a night when you woke up in the night amidst the darkness and wondered where you were. It was a strange habitation that gave birth to strange feelings.

Before the sun rose, we had woken up from our mats in the goat's pen. Mum however did not sleep much for when I woke up, she was already awake with her hands on her jaw deep in thought of what to do next, which wind to ride on next, and to which destination. She was so worried about our father's whereabouts if she would see him again in the way the war had escalated. She sat up pensive for a greater part of the night as the guns boomed away in the direction of Owerri where we had left a couple of hours ago.

It was about 5 in the morning and the place was still in darkness. We had slept heavily because of the long walk from the village. Falling asleep was very easy and waking was very hard. By 5 am, we were roused up by Mum to prepare for what the day was going to offer as we had gotten accustomed to doing in the war.

A cockerel dutifully stood guard and insisted it was morning and time to wake up by her constant crowing. We woke but could not venture out because it was still dark. We stayed until the sun came up sufficiently and birds started chirping. As people came out of their houses, we too crawled out of the pen we stayed for the night to a bright sunny morning like goats and fowls.

There was excitement in the air we could not readily explain. Mum interacted with one who had given us his goat's pen to sleep in. It was then that her face lighted up and she came with a new fire in her eyes that lighted us too. It was that the war had ended ingloriously for us. As a people, our course for self-determination scuttled.

Biafra had finally capitulated. The superior firepower of the federal army had ensured it. It was all over as we were told. The conflict of three years just came to an end overnight while we slumbered.

It was largely incredible and a point to raise eyebrows. I ran out to the main square and saw the victorious federal army. They had come into the town and were running around very close to where we stayed.

In the market, a stone's throw from where we stayed, some jubilant federal soldiers shot sporadically into the air. As I continued to watch the spectacle, something caught my fancy. A young woman was being dragged away by one soldier against her will. She refused to bow to the coercion of the soldier. She resisted with all her might as the soldier dragged her away. Her refusal also hardened the resolve of the soldier who took out his gun and fired at a point inches from the girl's toes. The bullet bore a hole in the ground by the girl's feet amidst heavy sparks of fire

I have seen enough. I ran back to where the pen was. I did not want to see any more abnormality. The soldiers were all over the area in a state of victory. No one dared oppose them. The girl's resistance was puerile. So was our resistance too. The soldiers rejoiced over our weakness and did whatever pleased them including taking spoils.

The war has ended. So we were told. We were still alive and still had a place we came from. Mum said it was time to go home. It was a long way home.

We were somehow elated about the end of the war to care about the distance home. It however marked a turning point in all our lives. We got together our things and thanked our host who was lost momentarily in incredulity and reality about the war's end.

He was still in this dazed mood when we stepped into the bright morning sunshine and into a new beginning for our impoverished lives that had been graciously spared.

The road was filled with refugees who were also going home because of the war's end. As we walked home, our morale was very low and our esteem as a people was reduced to the lowest level.

We set off for the long walk home with great fear of what the future held for us. The initial euphoria of the war's end has ended, like the morning dew that the emergence of the sun-dried out, so was ours. It dawned upon us that we had lost a war. The treatment meted to losers was what we awaited with great trepidation and uncertainty. We walked with our heads bowed in great sorrow, regret, and fear.

People were still dropping dead as we moved on despite the war's end. A boy my age could no longer walk and was left by her mother by the side of the road. There were lots of properties their owners could no longer carry. They jettisoned them like a plane in distress would jettison its excess fuel.

So, as we walked home, we saw lots of things thrown away as they lay strewn by the side of the road. One could see even babies, young boys and girls like me who could no longer walk and had become too heavy to be carried along by their mothers and those that carried them. These were left by the roadside to their fate while their people matched on to the future without them. These children looked very frail as they were abandoned to a terrible fate. It was indeed macabre.

I have never seen a survival story than the one that played out before me. We saw those that had died and those that were dying, their speculation focused beyond us and unto nothingness as they lay by the road on the way home. It was so painful when one was in the realization that the war had just ended and those that died today had to. It was not a good day or time to die immediately after a conflict. We matched on nonetheless in addition to a hastily contrived sigh.

On the main Okigwe/Owerri road, there were no vehicles but an unending stream of miserable, tattered and hungry looking refugees with heads bowed and walking home in utter shame of defeat. The only vehicles that ran on the roads were military trucks; their diesel-powered engines still audible in the far distance after they had passed. The place was otherwise quiet.

Jubilant and excited federal soldiers hung upon them and sang songs of jubilation that could be likened to the excitement of a game of soccer. They looked down on us like we were vermin, miserable, and a wretched lot.

Indeed, we looked like it. We had just lost a war and had the look of them that were vanquished in real terms. The soldiers rode on in excitement and triumph and they made it obvious. We could not look up to them, however. We were too humbled and fearful to behold their victorious faces. An incident took place as we walked home.

A man in his late thirties walked along with his children and wife. Their tattered belongings perched on their heads as they walked miserably along. And so, it was that a military truck came lumbering along. This man in other to appease our conquerors as they victoriously rode by, raised his hands, waved, greeted, and shouted at the top of his voice 'One Nigeria'. A soldier in the truck quickly retorted 'Shut up Biafra.' The man quickly shut up as was ordered. He felt very afraid and ashamed at this rebuke. He sulked away into the crowd of refugees as we walked home.

It confirmed our fears of what lay ahead of us as those who lost a major conflict. We became more aware of what to expect and stayed away from overreaching ourselves on this day of the victory of our enemies.

And so we trudged on, we got to where we slept a night earlier. We laughed at our changing fortunes and moved on closer to the home we left a night earlier.

We did not go through the city of Owerri. We avoided Owerri town because of the unforeseen and because of heavy roadblocks mounted by fierce and unfriendly-looking soldiers. So, we took to the paths.

Some of the sections of the path were not even better. It was littered with dead bodies with bullet wounds judging from openings on their bodies and others. Some others of sheer exhaustion as they lay in obedience to death.

So, we had in addition to our walk that was already encumbered an added task of moving away from dead bodies that littered the roads and paths to our village. It was horrifying.

In the face of all these, we counted ourselves lucky to be alive and spared. Chinwe's loss and my uncle's death were our only casualties.

We still did not know what lay ahead of us as we walked home. The sun still shined brightly above us. The wind blew and rustled the foliage on both sides of the lonely path with dead bodies. Birds still clattered noisily on both sides of the path. Everything else was normal.

The serenity of nature around us was such that it belied the graveness and death that lay all around us.

Our joy even in the face of the end of the war was greatly subdued. One could still be killed even in the unfolding euphoria of the end of the war. So, we walked home with certain trepidation at the quietness around us. This was why we took to the path ways to limit the dangers we faced on the main road.

On the last stretch to our village between Egbu and Naze, we started relaxing because we believed we had passed all the dangers and were not going to witness any other obstacles.

The conflict of many months had just ended and we were alive to see this very crucial turning point in our lives. We doubted the war's end. It was too good to be true. But with a tinge, we took the information. Does it mean that we were no longer going to see the planes that struck so much terror upon us? These flew over our huts at midday and dropped their oblong-shaped bombs upon our thatched roofs, setting them on fire. We were smoked out as rats with our blood pouring out on the earth as our limbs writhed lifeless on the ground.

It does also mean that we would sleep with our two eyes closed now. The very thing that had eluded us for three years and which had become our daily unobtrusive companion had suddenly departed. We were so used to them that it needed some convincing to make us believe that it was as we were experiencing or told that it was indeed all over.

However, in light of this situation-induced uncertainty, we counted ourselves extremely lucky to be walking home alive and well.

But other things stood and waited for us that we did not know about. In front of us was a roadblock manned by fierce-looking federal soldiers. Their unfriendly faces stared back at us without any change in their expression. Their kola nut-stained teeth showed how desperate the situation was. It was a surprise seeing them in the middle of nowhere and on the pathway to our home.

They stopped us and routinely searched us. They collected the red transistor I carried all along throughout the war. The soldier looked into my bucket that was my burden and the red transistor caught his fancy. He immediately went for it and brought it up. He looked at it and kept it behind him on top of the log that formed the checking post. He told me to move on after searching me.

That was how he collected the transistor that I had the responsibility of carrying all through the times we were running. He thoroughly searched for weapons and other things only he knew, and found none. What was he expecting to find in the kitty of an 9-year-old boy?

When they finally finished searching us all, they were about to let us go when something else caught their fancy. It was my mum.

My mother was young at 36 years of age; she was still young and was given to being of some beauty and freshness. She was not ugly in any consideration despite the shaving of her hair that was done to fade her beauty. She had a certain grace that made her very good to look at. Her nose was in between being snubbed and pointed. That put her at an obvious angle of being beautiful. Her eyes were elegantly and symmetrically placed in between her head.

From this point, Mother's eyes shined with some brightness that was alluring and as well as dazzling. Her gait was firm and purposeful. It was these that made the soldier notice her.

And so, it was that the soldier sighted her like one that had sighted an emerald on a certain enchanted shore. He called her to come, looked her over in one lustful glare, and asked her to stay at his back. The soldier with his kola nut-stained teeth barked at us to move on.

We had expressed our gratitude to God for keeping us safe all through the war. We had counted ourselves lucky to be alive and making it home in one piece on the day the war ended. How could this be, that our mother, at such a short distance to our home, was taken from us by enemy soldiers in pursuit of their selfish and lustful desires? She had been the source of our strength and what could our lives be without her?

And there she stood in the grips of a heartless captivity, beyond our very limited powers. She stared helplessly at us from behind the soldier who held her as we made to leave her behind. This was above her powers. She could not wriggle out of this situation as she had always done in the conflict and in the past. There she stood and stared with bewilderment and utter helplessness like one in a deep pit as we made to go on and leave her behind, there being no other thing either of us could do.

Mum had been our hero all along. She maneuvered us all out of trouble in the entire war even from the outset of it. She had been the reason why the family moved on and like a heroine, we all had acknowledged her as such. She was the epitome of strength. Even our father's influence was nothing compared to the much Mum wielded in the family. I never believed she could ever come to a position of weakness as she stared at us thoroughly emasculated and weakened beyond my imagination.

We had reluctantly accepted our overall fate at Mum's seizure by the soldier as their spoil. With tearful eyes, she looked at us as we turned to go away leaving her there.

My mother's elder sister, Dorothy was walking home with us. Her marriage failed. She was my mother's closest sister. She came to stay with us at times. We branched and collected her as we were coming home from Ogwa. This was how she came to be part of our troupe as we walked home.

We called her 'Nda Dora,' 'Dora' being the shortened form of Dorothy. Nda Dora was an amiable aunt of ours. She was very wise and approached issues from the wisdom that she had gained over the years. She loved my mother very much and was tilted towards her more than their eldest.

So, she saw us grow up and witnessed almost all the things we witnessed in the war. She was not as flamboyant as my mum. She was conservative and this dictated also her worldview.

And so, as the situation unfolded before us and she beheld it, spoke to us in the vernacular, "nne nu aladila."

So, what she told us meant that your mother has gone. This was a rally or a clarion for us. She further coaxed us into crying, that we should not move any more inches.

As kids, we were immuned to harassment and generally worked with the understanding that nothing could harm us. So, we stood before the soldiers and started wailing even with their mounted 'APMG' (All-purpose machine gun) pointed towards us. My elder brother Chika started crying first. He did not waste any time and theatrically started wailing with tears all over his young face. I joined in the melee and my eldest too joined in this action to embarrass and possibly rescue our mother by this.

We all started crying seriously before the soldiers. Tears filled our eyes and poured on the dry earth. It was a sorry sight to behold, three children crying helplessly over their mother who was in trouble. The particular soldier in question felt very embarrassed and blurted out to my mother who was by his side,

"Na your pikin"?

In Pidgin English.

Mum quickly nodded in the affirmative. The soldiers looked at themselves with confused glances. The one who had taken Mum told her "oya, oya, follow them".

That was how the man out of his embarrassment asked her to follow us and go. Mum quickly left them and came over to our side, to freedom, our waiting arms extended to have her back. We left the place fast and broke into a trot and soon lost sight of them.

What if it did not work out and they held on to mum? I could not bring myself to think of the prospects of life without her at that age we needed her most to face the world. It would have only come from the crucibles of cruel fate if she was separated from us a day after the war ended.

We were spared the agony of losing our mother by sheer providence. How about those who were not so lucky, who were not given any chance to plead or ask for a reprieve but were cut down by the guns that hounded us to early and reluctant graves? These looked on and saw calamity befall one or two of their members.

A case in point was the family that all died as we came out on the journey to safety. They were like us full of hopes and expectations for the future especially about surviving the senseless war. They were cut down altogether, with their thoughts and dreams.

We had been through thick and thin together and she had been the best of mothers. It could have only been providence that saw us through. I am very grateful.

We finally got home with subdued silence. The house was broken into as my uncle had threatened. Our bed sheet was stolen and our cat was also killed by my uncle. When confronted, he said that the cat was wild. It was the least of what calamity we expected. It did not matter much in so far as we were all alive.

It was reasoned that another bedsheet could always be bought and another cat got. The most important thing was that we were alive. It did not matter much what was lost. What mattered was the fact that God had made it so that we were not killed like many who died. Let my uncle take the cat and the sheets.

The incident at the checkpoint sobered Mum up in no small way. She came to the understanding that indeed anything could happen. It was learned that anything could happen at very short notice. It remarkably changed her worldview. She did not hold on to things tenaciously from then on. She learned to let go more easily.

A new era had begun no matter how we disliked or liked it. We were unprepared for these times of peace and tranquility. The times of war were not expected to end so soon though we were tired of the war. But the times suddenly changed and we were caught off guard. It was like them in the dark who had to contend with a sudden burst of light.

We shielded our eyes from this brightness and waited to get accustomed to it again.

The life we were forced to live these past days which we got accustomed to had gone suddenly. The sound of gunfire and the boom of guns had fallen silent.

The greatest cheery news of the war's end was that it ended unexpectedly. It was the reason why the news was greeted with great incredulity.

Our homestead was no longer what it used to be. It could not be, with the dead and the empty places they left. These served as a grim reminder of the conflict that inflicted wounds and hurt on us beyond anything, we had experienced in our entire lives. Our number and strength were reduced. Our productivity was affected and seriously hampered if not crippled.

Things changed so fast. Such things as her white bicycle, which she suffered to retrieve from Dyke, and her box of wrappers were all brought out again. The threat of their being appropriated was no longer there. It was however so comforting that it had come to this.

As the boxes were brought out, it was painfully discovered that the wrappers became unusable. They tore at a very little tug. The whole effort at preserving it was wasted. But it was overcome by the lone fact that the war had ended. This made it at least bearable.

It was futile counting the cost. What happened had to be spared only a fleeting glance. Those who died could not come back to life to speculate. The opportunities that came and went in those three years of course could never be known and could never be recalled.

The men that went in defense of their fatherland came home. One after another they sauntered home. Some with wounds and others without any as they sadly came home. Some had their hands disfigured and some had broken legs that enabled them to limp home, while some came home without a scratch. Such people like my uncle, Chukwe came home whole.

They brought News with them of those of our kin that were not coming home again. They furnished us with information and the circumstances that led to their untimely death. It was painful, to say the least of how we all felt.

Even my mother's two brothers could not make it out of the war alive. They died fighting in defense of their father's land having answered the clarion call. It was a lot of wishful thinking. 'What if they were around' we found ourselves wishing.

I was nine years old. I was seeing things from a better perspective and not from the fuzziness of a child's view. I was better apprised of what was going on now than when the war started. No one was spared of sorrow in those days. But anyhow, we geared up to pick up the pieces. The future still lay ahead of us.

Life did not change automatically but wobbled on in this era of quieter times devoid of boom of guns and frightening roars of fighter jets that made our hearts pound on our chest. Our old routine got restarted devoid of threats to our lives. Our meals graciously assumed a more interesting dimension. It became salted.

If Chinwe had made it out, it would have excited her that salt came again especially. We still ate yam porridge but not as was the case in the war, the boring and monotonous food we constantly ate. But there was a promise of better days as the conflict had ended.

It was made even more reassuring with the three R R R (Reconstruction, Rehabilitation, and Re-integration) proclaimed by the federal government under Yakubu Gowon. We believed that it was going to be better and that only God had indeed spared us.

CHAPTER 12

WHY BIAFRA LOST THE WAR

According to Mazi K. Ani of the Civil Rights League) in his article (why Biafra lost), it was made quite clear why we could not win the war as hoped. Firstly, he opined that Biafra lost mainly because the idea that it portrayed was far too advanced for its time. The Biafran war broke out six years after Nigeria's independence.

At that time anti-colonial struggles were still going on elsewhere in Africa, pitting African nationalists against colonial and neo-colonial forces in countries such as Angola, Mozambique, Zimbabwe, South Africa, etc. The issues thrown up by Biafra had not been understood at the time as they are now.

Also, another reason adduced by Mazi k. Ani (why Biafra lost the war) were issues about self-determination against territorial integrity. According to him, the dominant debate was the right of states to maintain their territorial integrity. At the time of Biafra, the principle of territorial integrity was upheld worldwide over self-determination. And because the Nigerian side represented the politically correct ideology at the time, it was able to mobilize a vast array of forces incorporating both NATO and Warsaw Pact countries and the Arab League (USSR, UK, OAU, USA, EGYPT, etc.) against Biafra which was seen as a threat to Nigeria's territorial integrity.

At the time Biafra was declared, very few people example France's Charles de Gaulle, Tanzania's Julius Nyerere, Zambia's Kenneth Kaunda, etc. upheld the right of nations to self-determination over territorial integrity of states. Today the picture is different. The scale has tipped in favour of national self-determination as seen in Eritrea, Yugoslavia, East Timor, USSR, etc. against Biafra which was seen as an abhorrent threat to Nigeria's territorial integrity.

Indeed, during the Biafran period, the collapse of any state was viewed with utmost horror. He further said that Yakubu Gowon scored a cheap point by raising the specter of tens of African republics invading the UN for self-determination demands. No one imagined that the big and powerful USSR would disappear from the world map, with each of its 15 constituent republics becoming full members of the UN and the high heavens did not fall.

Today the reality of the collapse of national territories is taken for granted after the disintegration of the USSR, Czechoslovakia, Yugoslavia, and separatist pressures in Canada, Spain, and Britain, etc.

Also, Mazi Ani opined that Biafra's attempt to challenge in the 1960s the viability of the African boundaries as constituted by colonial powers was one of the reasons why it did not win the war. At the time, the received wisdom was that African boundaries were inviolable and non-negotiable. The idea was that if these boundaries were challenged successfully, it would open a flood gates for more agitations and therefore chaos in Africa and everywhere else.

As a result, the OAU incorporated in its charter, the inviolability of African boundaries of the already existing states, a clause which it defended with great zeal.

This was the principle which Biafra attempted to challenge in the 60s. This idea was obviously far ahead of its time. Today after millions of Africans have died in wars related to these same boundaries, millions are maimed and millions more rendered homeless, serious people everywhere have come to see the futility of maintaining those artificial boundaries.

Many more Africans have died fighting about Africa's artificial boundaries that were killed under direct European colonialism itself.

For example, when the British colonial police shot a dozen coal miners in Enugu, all hell broke loose but the Biafra war claimed millions of lives.

The same scenario played out in Rwanda, Burundi, Congo, etc. Therefore a lot more people are willing to accept that African boundaries are not and should not be inviolable.

Ironically, Ethiopia presided over Biafra and became the first to accept this compelling reality by not only letting Eritrea go but by also incorporating the right to secession in its constitution.

The OAU has lost much of its relevance and become a talking shop for tin-pot dictators, no longer able or willing to assert the principle of inviolable and sacrosanct boundaries.

Also, the Biafra war strategy was based on the goodness of the international community and their ability to intervene in the resolution of conflicts. Biafra believed that the international community would not stand by while acts of genocide were being committed. Again, this idea was far ahead of its time. It was not until the 1990s in Rwanda, Somalia, Bosnia, and Kosovo that the international community became involved in this way. At the time of Biafra, the international community was there all right but there was no unity of purpose between the wishes of the masses and those of their government.

Thus, while the masses and their organizations in Europe and North America i.e. charities funded by mass donations supported Biafra, their governments supported the Nigerian side. Nigeria's argument that other states should not interfere in her internal affairs was more or less accepted by the international community, except the aid agencies.

Today the situation is different in that governments can, according to the humanitarian impulse of the masses prevent international disasters of the Biafran scale, territorial integrity or no territorial integrity, and internal or no internal affairs as seen recently in Kosovo.

Another question that was thrown up by the Biafran struggle which was poorly understood at that time was the religious undertone in it.

Although the conflict between Christianity and Islam is a very old one, at the time of the Biafran conflict, the main ideological struggle was between communism and capitalism. Biafra however presented the religious side of the conflict to the world but again on this issue, Biafra was far ahead of its time. Whereas Biafra saw the struggle as one between Islam and Christianity, the Nigerian side was able to use Yakubu Gowon and Anthony Enahoro to mask the religious dimensions of the war.

With the end of the Cold War and the emergence of Islamic fundamentalism worldwide threatening the interest of the U S. and European states, the religious issue is viewed rather differently today. The re-emergence of the sharia etc. In Nigeria, al Qaeda and Islamic international-sponsored terrorism today, show a far clearer understanding of the question than was possible at the time of Biafra.

Also, in contention according Mazi Ani, the concept of Hausa Fulani hegemony and the role of local groups played a decisive in the case against Biafra.

Apart from the international ideological currency of maintaining the territorial integrity of existing states at the time of Biafra, the other major reason for Biafra's defeat was the role of local groups. Biafra interpreted the conflict in north-south terms, internal colonialism, and the need to fight Hausa Fulani domination.

This idea turned out to be ahead of its time in that many local groups did not buy the idea of northern domination. Indeed, many local groups contested the notion of Hausa Fulani domination and considered Igbo domination as a more dangerous threat to themselves.

This explained the pattern of alliance that occurred during the war, the idea of northern domination was brought only by a radical fringe made up of Wole Soyinka, Tai Solarin, etc., and was of no mobilizing value.

In the mid-west, the idea of northern domination was rejected by all non-Igbo groups who considered Igbo domination to be far more dangerous. In eastern Nigeria, not only was Hausa Fulani domination rejected, but the non-Igbo groups saw Hausa Fulani as liberators from Igbo domination.

Again, Biafra lost the war because we were outgunned and outmanned by the Nigerian side. As a result of the international climate that existed at the time of Biafra, the Nigerian side was able to put together a more formidable array of forces that eventually gave them more military clout that led to the fall of Biafra.

That international configuration of ideologies and forces has now shifted. With all the foregoing, it will not be that the whole world would sit by today and watch Nigeria murder 2 million Igbos as was the case in 1967-70. This is a fact.

With all the power that social media these days have, it would be preposterous to think that the international community would look the other way while such events as happened in the days of Biafra would dare repeat themselves.

So, it is believed that the local attitudinal atmosphere or climate also appears to have changed in such a way that will make it impossible to recreate the anti-Biafran alliance of 1967.

The 'sabo' syndrome was another cankerworm that contributed to the eating away of the efforts at letting Biafra stand. This word 'sabo' came from the word 'saboteur', a word that defines one intentionally helping a potential enemy.

This played out in the case of Banjo's foray of the Biafran army into the Midwest and southwest in the war. In those days, I was aware of the devasting effects this had on the outcome of the war. The war efforts were sabotaged for some reasons I am not sure of but for pecuniary consideration. If the Biafran soldiers had sustained their push into the west of the country in the war, it would have changed the outcome of the war willy-nilly in favour of Biafra.

BIBILIOGRAPHY

1. Achebe, Chinua, (2012) There was a Country; A personal history of Biafra; Penguin

2. Aghalino, S.O. British Colonial Policies and The Oil palm Industry in The Niger Delta Region of Nigeria, 1900-1960. African Study monographs 21(i), 2000, 19-33

3. Ani k. (Mazi). (A Riposte to Revisionism) CIVIL RIGHTS LEAGUE NIG.

4. Anthony, A. Douglas; Poison and Medicine, Ethnicity, power and violence in a Nigerian city, 1966/1986. Oxford.

5. Awoyokun, Damola; 'The Untold Story of Nigeria's civil war' P M News (19th february.2013)

6. Bible. Mathew 2;18. Proverbs 31;27.

7. Chinweizu, I. A public lecture delivered at the Agip recital hall, center, Onikan Lagos on 18th February, 2006.

8. Chukwuemeka, V. Ike; Sunset at Dawn; A novel about Biafra. University press P L C. 1993.

9. David, Laitin. Hegemony and Cultures; Politics and Religious Change among the Yoruba's (1986) Chicago, The University of Chicago press.

10. Encyclopedia Britannica. Nigeria as a colony. 2002

11. Osuji, Steve. (23 October 2012) "There was a country; ogbunigwe, Abagana Ambush; Achebe, Okigbo, and I.feajuna. The Nation Online. Archived from the original on 18th Dec.2015.

12. Helleiner, G.k. (1967) Peasant Agriculture, Government and Economic Growth in Nigeria. Illinois; Homewood.

13. Melbourne. M, Roy; the American response to the Nigerian conflict, 1968; a journal of opinions; vol3.no 2. Summer 1973. Pp33-42

14. Ruth, First, The Barrel of a Gun; The Politics of coup d'état in Africa. (Allen lane. The penguin press, London, 1970.

15. Watts. Michael; Silent violence; food famine and peasantry in Northern Nigeria. University of California press.1983.

16. The problems of Nigerian Unity> the case of Northern Nigeria, page 28. Original memorandum submitted by the Eastern delegation to the Nigerian ad hoc constitutional conference which opened in Lagos on 12th September 1966.

17. Memorandum submitted by the Northern delegates to the Nigerian ad hoc constitutional conference. Lagos, 12th September, 1966.

18. Report of the justice G.C.M Onyiuke Tribunal (toll brook limited, ikeja, Lagos)

19. William, Shakespeare, Macbeth. Publishers; Edward Blount and William Jaggard. 1629